a devotional journal

I Praise You Because...

Patti Wiens

CMC PUBLISHING
Mora Minnesota

Design by Creative Marketing Concepts, Inc. (CMC)

Senior Designer Anthony Alex LeTourneau

Editor Leah Spieler

Assisting Editors Julie Kolodji, Gabriel McKay and Anna Carlson

First Printing July 2005

Printed in India

ISBN 0-9761408-1-0

Author's Dedication

To everyone who reads this book...
may you discover, as I have, how very awesome
a FATHER-GOD we have as His children.

A special thanks to Sandy Kaye Pearson,
who never stopped encouraging me
to write this devotional book,
and whose expertise made it come about,
and to Marlene Johnson,
my colleague in education and my friend,
who spent hours proofing this book.

foreword

by Fred Carlson, *Publisher*

The most valuable days of my life have consistently been those that begin with a quiet devotional time of praise to God. Those days are not necessarily void of problems, but they are rich with an energy of peace. As I praise God, I become infused with the strength of His Holy Spirit. God inhabits the praise of His people. In this way, the Lord gives me the spiritual guts and fabric sufficient for the day. I'm able to stand and confidently endure challenges and disappointments because I have gained the needed portion of God's perspective. I praise Him for that!

One will quickly notice that Patti's prayers of praise are written from the perspective of a committed Christian—someone seeking to know God better each day. Through praising Him for who He is, you, too, will surely find enrichment and fullness not known by any other means.

I find it disappointing that today, many Christian speakers and writers focus only on believing and receiving in their walk with God, rather than the foundational requirements of trusting and obeying. I appreciate that Patti recognizes the spiritual necessity of both.

Please attempt to take time to journal, even if it is only in sentence fragments. Journaling is a way of expression back to God from your heart. The act of recording our thoughts, emotions, and circumstances of the day is extremely therapeutic. It helps establish in our hearts and minds the hope that God provides us as a result of offering our praises to Him.

The dinner table for the scriptural enrichment of your life has been set before you in the form of this devotional journal. May the Holy Spirit Himself indwell you as you read the Old and New Testament Scriptures and express praises for your Lord. Enjoy. Be filled. Praise God.

Day 1

...You are the Creator of all.

In the beginning God created the heavens and the earth.
Genesis 1:1 (NIV)

Today's Truth:
God is the Creator of all, the Master
Architect of the universe.

Creator:
maker
designer

Prayer of Praise

God, You are responsible for all the wonders of creation... the
mountains so majestic that they take my breath away, the oceans, the
animals that instinctively care for their young, the birds, the fish of the
seas, the lakes, the forests, and all of mankind. These are wonders of
Your creative power. God, You can do anything! Great are You, Lord,
and greatly to be praised for all You have created and will continue to
create for my pleasure and for Your glory. Amen.

Personal Meditation

Day 2

...You are the Preserver.

God didn't forget about Noah and all the animals in the boat! He sent a wind to blow across the waters, and the floods began to disappear, for the subterranean water sources ceased their gushing, and the torrential rains subsided. Genesis 8:1-2 (LB)

As long as the earth remains, there will be springtime and harvest, cold and heat, winter and summer, day and night. Genesis 8:22 (LB)

Today's Truth:

God preserves His children. Through all the storms of life He guards and keeps each one.

Preserve:

keep in safety
guard
keep intact

Prayer of Praise

I praise You because You safely guard me. In prayer You always meet me. You defend and protect me. I praise You because I'm secure in You. You are my shield. You uphold me and direct my feet on the right path that will lead me to Your house. Amen.

Personal Meditation

Day 3

...You are the Promise-Giver.

And God said, "This is the sign of the covenant I am making between me and you and every living creature with you, a covenant for all generations to come: I have set my rainbow in the clouds, and it will be the sign of the covenant between me and the earth... I will remember my covenant between me and you and all living creatures of every kind. Never again will the waters become a flood to destroy all life."
Genesis 9:12-13, 15 (NIV)

Today's Truth:
God's promises never fail. He is always and forever true to His Word.

Promise:
vow
pledge
guarantee

Prayer of Praise

I praise You because Your promises give me hope. Your promises provide that longed-for state of happiness in being able to come boldly into Your presence and share my deepest joys, sorrows and needs. Amen.

Personal Meditation

Day 4

...You are the Scatterer.

So the LORD scattered them from there over all the earth,
and they stopped building the city.
Genesis 11:8 (NIV)

Today's Truth:
The Lord moves His people in ways we may not understand, but we can always trust His motive.

Scatter:
disperse
separate in different directions

Prayer of Praise

I praise You for sending Your children in different directions. You disperse some of us into our own neighborhoods, while You send others to sow the seed of Your love in distant places. Father, You are the Giver of everlasting life. Please help me to see the opportunities that arise each day to share Your good news with others, that they may come to know You. Amen.

Personal Meditation

Day 5

...You are the Supreme God.

And blessed be God Most High, who delivered
your enemies into your hand...
Genesis 14:20a (NIV)

Today's Truth:
God has the ultimate authority
and victory over every
imaginable problem.

Supreme:
highest
foremost
ultimate

Prayer of Praise

I praise You, Lord–You Who are highest in power...You Who are
foremost in authority. To realize that the Almighty Supreme God
loves me and counts me as precious in His sight is beyond my
understanding! Thank You for loving me...You Who are the First and
the Last...and the Greatest! Amen.

Personal Meditation

...You are the God of heaven and earth.

Acknowledge and take to heart this day that the LORD is God in heaven above and on the earth below. There is no other.
Deuteronomy 4:39 (NIV)

Today's Truth:

The LORD is God of all
and has commanded that I
acknowledge Him.

Acknowledge:

recognize
accept
confess

Prayer of Praise

God Almighty, I am in awe of Your magnificent creation. As I gaze at the marvels of heaven and earth, I do so in wonder. Your handiwork can be seen in Arizona'a deserts, Switzerland's Alps, Wyoming's geysers, Alaska's glaciers, the Amazon River and the Grand Canyon. You are Lord of all that is in heaven and on earth. You are my God and I praise You. Amen.

Personal Meditation

Day 7

...You are the God who blesses.

Your descendants will be like the dust of the earth, and you will spread
out to the west and to the east and to the north and to the south.
All peoples on earth will be blessed through you and your offspring.
Genesis 28:14 (NIV)

Today's Truth:

God's plan is for His children to
be blessed and for His children to
be a blessing to all.

Bless:

to give divine favor

Prayer of Praise

I praise You for granting me Your divine favor through Your blessings.
Father, I cherish Your countless gifts: health...peace...family...
America...eyes that see...ears that hear...the Bible...Christian
friends...warmth in winter...food to eat...my salvation. Your blessings
are as many as the stars on a cloudless night! Through Your blessings I
receive great joy. This moment, I praise You from the depths of my soul
for all my blessings. Amen.

Personal Meditation

...You are the God who turns evil to good.

But Joseph said to them, "Do not be afraid, for am I in God's place?
As for you, you meant evil against me, but God meant it for good..."
Genesis 50:19-20a (NASB)

Today's Truth:

God chooses and is able to use
even the bad in our lives for good.

Goodness:

that which is positive, desirable
and beneficial

Prayer of Praise

I praise You for being the God who took my sinful, depraved life
and turned it into something beautiful. Father, at times there are
circumstances and people that would bring harm to me. Yet You
influence the outcomes, making them virtuous and of great value in
my life. Your Word produces in me moral excellence and good
deeds—all because of You. Amen.

Personal Meditation

Day 9

...You are the Sovereign God.

God said to Moses, "I AM WHO I AM"; and He said, "Thus you shall say to the sons of Israel, 'I AM has sent me to you.'" God, furthermore, said to Moses, "Thus you shall say to the sons of Israel, 'The LORD, the God of your fathers, the God of Abraham, the God of Isaac, and the God of Jacob, has sent me to you.' This is My name forever, and this is My memorial-name to all generations."
Exodus 3:14-15 (NASB)

Today's Truth:
God has, and will always have, the final word.

Sovereign:
exercises supreme judgement and power

Prayer of Praise

I praise You for possessing supreme power. Father, there is no other god like You. Your sovereignty is excellent...Your sovereignty is great...Your sovereignty is exalted far above the heavens. My mind cannot take in that You see all, know all, are everywhere at once...and yet by Your Holy Spirit You live within me. Oh, Father God, how can this be?! Amen.

Personal Meditation

Day 10

...You are the Lord, who is my Strength, Song, and Salvation.

The LORD is my strength and song, And He has become my salvation; This is my God, and I will praise Him; My father's God, and I will extol Him.
Exodus 15:2 (NASB)

Today's Truth:

The Lord is the muscle, the music, and the very means of my salvation. He is life itself.

Salvation:

deliverance from sin
redemption

Prayer of Praise

I praise You because You are my melodious utterance...my song in the night; my song in the light; my song of absolute delight. Father, Your salvation delivers me from evil, danger, even ruin. You are my strength when I falter and fail. You are my strength in crisis and need. How can I do anything but praise You? Amen.

Personal Meditation

Day 11

...You are a wonder-working God.

Who among the gods is like you, O LORD? Who is like you—
majestic in holiness, awesome in glory, working wonders?
Exodus 15:11 (NIV)

Today's Truth:
No one compares to God
Almighty. His being and His acts
are awesome.

Wonder:
miracle
marvel
phenomenon

Prayer of Praise

Precious Father, I stand in awe of:
    the wonder of my salvation,
    the strength of Your unconditional love,
    the beauty of the world around me,
    the mystery of what You are preparing for me in heaven.

Father, I come to You today with astonishment and admiration, laced
and mingled with surprise at a wonder-working God! Amen.

Personal Meditation

Day 12

...You are a God of splendor and holiness.

Who else is like the Lord among the gods?
Who is glorious in holiness like him?
Who is so awesome in splendor, a wonder-working God?
Exodus 15:11 (LB)

Today's Truth:

There is none like You–
Awesome God!

Splendor:

magnificent greatness

Prayer of Praise

Father, though I cannot grasp entirely Your "awesome splendor", I do give You praise. Today I see Your greatness in a life given to You, in a baby being born, and even in the health and strength I enjoy. No one but You can create and maintain all that is about me. Your absolute holiness is unfathomable. Amen.

Personal Meditation

Day 13

...Your sovereign authority will never end.

The LORD will reign for ever and ever.
Exodus 15:18 (NIV)

Today's Truth:

God's authority, love and power
will not fade or pass away.

Reign:
hold and exercise
sovereign power

Prayer of Praise

Father, those words "forever and ever" bring total comfort and peace.
Earthly governmental bodies come and go. Policies change. We scurry
about in an uncertain world, but You remain. Amen.

Personal Meditation

Day 14

...You deeply love those who walk with You.

*...but I lavish my love upon thousands of those who love me
and obey my commandments.*
Exodus 20:6 (LB)

Today's Truth:

My heavenly Father's love is
generously given to me.

Lavish:

to give generously

Prayer of Praise

Extravagantly...Profusely...Generously...Bountifully...
Father, all these words describe how You lavish Your love upon me.
To realize You heap Your love upon me with no restraint...
Oh, how I praise You! Amen.

Personal Meditation

Day 15

...You are the Lord my God.

...and they shall know that I am the Lord their God.
I brought them out of Egypt so that I could live among them.
I am Jehovah their God.
Exodus 29:46 (LB)

Today's Truth:

My Lord walks with me
and I can know Him.

Lord:

one who possesses supreme
power and authority

Prayer of Praise

I praise You because You are the Lord; You are my God. Just as You led
Israel out of Egypt, so today, Father, be my leader....
guide me, protect me, direct me. How I praise You for loving me and
directing my steps through difficult circumstances as well as the joyous
times. Amen.

Personal Meditation

Day 16

...You are always near.

I am always thinking of the Lord; and because he is so near,
I never need to stumble or to fall.
Psalm 16:8 (LB)

Today's Truth:

My Lord walks with me –
I need not fall.

Stumble:

speak or act wrongly

Prayer of Praise

I praise You, Father, for Your constant, steadying Presence in my life.
As each day begins, and as each draws to a close, You are beside me.
Your Word is in my heart and mind. Please give me Your thoughts
today, so I will glorify You in what I say and do. Amen

Personal Meditation

...You are slow to anger.

*And he passed in front of Moses, proclaiming, "The LORD, the LORD,
the compassionate and gracious God,
slow to anger, abounding in love and faithfulness, maintaining love
to thousands, and forgiving wickedness, rebellion and sin..."
Exodus 34:6-7a (NIV)*

Today's Truth:

My God abounds in love
and mercy.

Merciful:

compassionate
forgiving
pardoning

Prayer of Praise

Father, I live in an angry world... where quick tempers, violence and
mistreatment are not uncommon. Oh how wonderful to come into Your
presence where there is love and grace. It brings me peace and comfort
to know that even though Your anger is perfect and totally justified, You
remain compassionate and enduring in grace. You do not lash out at me
in wrath, but rather You are gentle and loving and ever so patient with
all of my faults and failures. Father, I praise You for shaping me, not by
angry blows but by loving guidance and correction! Amen.

Personal Meditation

Day 18

...You cleanse us from all our sins.

I have told everyone the Good News that you forgive men's sins.
I have not been timid about it, as you well know, O Lord.
Psalm 40:9 (LB)

Today's Truth:

The Good News is that Christ, my Lord, has made the forgiveness of sins available to all people.

Forgive:

pardon, remit

Prayer of Praise

It is so wonderful, Father, to tell people that You want to forgive their sins and to carry their burdens! I love to tell of Your cleansing power! You not only forgive sins of today, but You have provided for the forgiveness of ALL sins– PAST, PRESENT, AND FUTURE– through the sacrifice of Christ! Amen

Personal Meditation

Day 19

...You are the Lord Who rescues.

Turn, O LORD, and deliver me; save me because of your unfailing love.
Psalm 6:4 (NIV)

Today's Truth:
My loving Lord will rescue me.

Rescue:
to save from danger
ransom
redeem

Prayer of Praise

I am sure I will not be fully aware today of all the ways You will rescue me. At obvious times of need, I feel and know Your uplifting hand of protection. I praise You for surrounding me, covering me and filling me with Your Holy Spirit... the One Who goes before me, behind me, above me, under me, but greatest of all, the One Who indwells me! Amen.

Personal Meditation

Day 20

...You equip me to do Your work.

God has filled them both with unusual skills as jewelers, carpenters, embroidery designers in blue, purple, and scarlet on linen backgrounds, and as weavers— they excel in all the crafts we will be needing in the work.
Exodus 35:35 (LB)

Today's Truth:
God will fully prepare me for
each task He gives me.

Prayer of Praise

I praise You, Father, because You are my equipper. You prepare me for each and every purpose and undertaking. Even as You gave special gifts to these Old Testament men to bring glory to You, so be glorified in the gifts You have bestowed upon me for the building of Your Kingdom. You alone know me through and through...when I sit, when I rise, before a word is on my tongue You know it completely! (Psalm 139) What an amazing and intimate God You are! Amen.

Personal Meditation

Day 21

...You, Lord, are holy.

You shall be holy to me, for I the Lord am holy,
and I have set you apart from all other peoples, to be mine.
Leviticus 20:26 (LB)

Today's Truth:
The Lord is my
righteousness.

Holy:
godly
pure
righteous

Prayer of Praise

Father, You have called me to be holy as You are holy. In every situation, may I ask, "What would Jesus do?" Oh, dear Lord Jesus, only in You can I attain to any level of holiness. You have given me Your breastplate of righteousness to wear each day, and so today I gladly put it on! Amen.

Personal Meditation

Day 22

...You are the LORD who sanctifies.

Do not profane my holy name. I must be acknowledged
as holy by the Israelites. I am the LORD, who makes you holy.
Leviticus 22:32 (NIV)

Today's Truth:

In Christ I can be pure.

Holy:

set apart to God

Prayer of Praise

I am amazed, Father God, that You set me apart for Your purpose and for Your glory. Because You cleansed me, I am released from the power sin had over me. Each day it is Your desire to purify me anew in my mind, my will, and my emotions. What an awesome Holy God You are. Amen.

Personal Meditation

_____

_____

_____

_____

_____

_____

_____

...You are a just God.

His ever-expanding, peaceful government will never end. He will rule
with perfect fairness and justice from the throne of his father David.
He will bring true justice and peace to all the nations of the world.
This is going to happen because the Lord of heaven's armies
has dedicated himself to do it!
Isaiah 9:7 (LB)

Today's Truth:

My Lord is the author of
justice and peace.

Justice:

fairness

Prayer of Praise

In a world of great injustice, Father, I praise You for Your absolute
fairness. We live today in an imperfect world of prejudice and
pride manifested in a thousand selfish ways. Only You can bring
the promised "peace to all nations". How Great Thou Art – in Your
Amazing Grace! Amen.

Personal Meditation

...You give me peace and take my fears away.

...for I will give you peace, and you will go to sleep without fear.
Leviticus 26:6a (LB)

Today's Truth:

Fear has no place in the rest God gives His children.

Peace:

calmness
tranquility

Prayer of Praise

How often in my childhood, Father, I prayed,
"Now I lay me down to sleep,
I pray the Lord my soul to keep..."
Even today as many years have come and gone, I praise You for Your promised rest. I know that as I rest in You, there is no room for the anxiety and turmoil that so quickly sap my energy. I praise You for Your promised protection and the peace it brings! Amen.

Personal Meditation

Day 25

...You are kind to those who love and obey You.

*...but I will show kindness to a thousand generations of those
who love me and keep my commandments.*
Deuteronomy 5:10b (LB)

Today's Truth:

As I trust and obey, Your
tender kindness is given
to me.

Kindness:

tenderness
affection

Prayer of Praise

Your favor lasts for a lifetime... how can I adequately praise You for the
depth of such affection to me? Thank You that Your awesome promises
extend beyond me – to my children and their children. I find great
assurance in the fact that if they choose to love and obey Your Word,
You will show Your gentleness and favor to them also. Amen.

Personal Meditation

Day 26

...You are my Forever Friend!

But God is my helper. He is a friend of mine!
Psalm 54:4 (LB)

Today's Truth:

God is my every moment
companion and friend.

Friend:

advocate
ally
companion

Prayer of Praise

I gladly bring You praise today, Father, for I cherish the friendship
You extend to me. You are One Who is even closer to me than my
own family. You rescue me and lift me up out of the despair and
discouragement of the night. You go ahead of me to guard and guide
my way. All You ask is that I hold Your hand. I can always depend upon
You. Amen.

Personal Meditation

Day 27

...Your love is magnificent and steadfast.

*Oh, I plead with you, pardon the sins of this people because of
your magnificent, steadfast love, just as you have forgiven them
all the time from when we left Egypt until now.*
Numbers 14:19 (LB)

Today's Truth:

God extends His perfect
love and forgiveness to
me this moment!

Magnificent:

lavish
exceptional
excellent

Prayer of Praise

Your love is exceptional, lavished upon me, and firmly fixed. How
wonderful is Your love. When I was not loved by my own, I turned to
You and I received Your love. I could fill pages with examples of how
Your love has been demonstrated in my life. It has been a constant
thread through the highs and lows. Even today, I know You love me
unconditionally. Amen.

Personal Meditation

...When I obey You, all is well with my soul.

Be careful to obey all these commandments. If you do what is right in the eyes of the Lord your God, all will go well with you and your children forever.
Deuteronomy 12:28 (LB)

Today's Truth:
With obedience comes
blessing.

Commandments:
orders
mandates

Prayer of Praise

Though I know that each of my children's path to You must be their own journey, how I praise You for the promise that when I am obedient, THEN life will go well for me and my children. I rest in that today, dear Father, because You are completely trustworthy. Amen.

Personal Meditation

...You do not leave me alone.

*For the Lord your God is merciful—he will not
abandon you nor destroy you nor forget the promises
he has made to your ancestors.*
Deuteronomy 4:31 (LB)

Today's Truth:

God walks with me
always.

Abandon:

desert
forsake
reject
leave behind

Prayer of Praise

Thank You, thank You for forgiveness and for Your forbearance toward
me. Your kindnesses to me are so plentiful. You restore me when I ask
for forgiveness... just as though I'd never sinned! The same mercy that
You gave to Israel long ago, You extend to me every day. Hallelujah,
what a Savior! Amen.

Personal Meditation

Day 30

...You are a God Who is alive!

*Then the angel spoke to the women, "Don't be frightened!" he said. "I
know you are looking for Jesus, who was crucified, but he isn't here!
For he has come back to life again, just as he said he would.
Come in and see where his body was lying.*
Matthew 28:5-6 (LB)

Today's Truth:

I serve a risen Savior!

Alive:

abounding in life
active
dynamic

Prayer of Praise

Though my eyes have not yet seen You, I am able to "see" you in my
spirit. Because You are alive, I too can live...forever with You. Today I
can walk in the reality of Your Holy Spirit's power. I do serve a risen
Savior, the God of the universe, Creator of all. One Who is alive and at
work in my life! Amen.

Personal Meditation

Day 31

...You are a great and awesome God.

Do not be terrified by them, for the LORD your God,
who is among you, is a great and awesome God.
Deuteronomy 7:21 (NIV)

Today's Truth:

My Lord God is greater
than all that threatens me.

Awesome:

fearsome
daunting
formidable

Prayer of Praise

Father, how immense and vast You are! You dwell in awesome
excellence. I stand in reverential awe of You today... deeply thankful
that You are holding my hand. In the rush of the day, the trials of the
hour, and even the sharp pain of the moment – You are with me. May
I walk today in keen awareness of Your capacity and greatness on my
behalf. I praise You for the confidence and assurance I find in You, my
Awesome God. Amen.

Personal Meditation

...You rescue us with a mighty hand.

I prayed to the LORD and said, "O Sovereign LORD,
do not destroy your people, your own inheritance that you redeemed
by your great power and brought out of Egypt with a mighty hand."
Deuteronomy 9:26 (NIV)

Today's Truth:
God has power to save and lift
us up.

Redeemed:
delivered
ransomed
bought back

Prayer of Praise

How deserving of glory You are, Father God! The intensity of Your
love, power and strength is glorious. You raise up and You bring
down... There is none like You! Thank You, Father, for delivering me
today from all that would press me down or crush my spirit. You are
indeed bigger than all my problems. As I go into my day, I know I can
rest in You. Amen.

Personal Meditation

Day 33

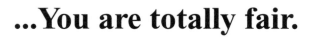

...You are totally fair.

*For the LORD your God is God of gods and Lord of lords,
the great God, mighty and awesome, who shows no partiality
and accepts no bribes.*
Deuteronomy 10:17 (NIV)

Today's Truth:
God will not play
favorites.

Partiality:
favoritism

Prayer of Praise

In this selfish world of bias, Father God, I praise You for being
incorruptible. In You there is no variableness. You do not favor one of
Your children above another, nor do You grade me on performance. I'm
so thankful that You look beyond my faults and failures and instead see
me through the loving eyes of Jesus Christ! Amen.

Personal Meditation

Day 34

...You concern Yourself with justice for those whom the world overlooks.

He gives justice to the fatherless and widows. He loves foreigners
and gives them food and clothing.
Deuteronomy 10:18 (LB)

Today's Truth:
God's love and fairness
reaches out to every person.

Justice:
fairness
equity

Prayer of Praise

Today, Father God, I praise You because You are, always and forever,
concerned about the needs of destitute children, widows, single
parents, and strangers in a new land. You care for each one... for every
heart that has a burden – You care! And that includes me! I give You
my heartfelt praise. Amen.

Personal Meditation

Day 35

...You are THE ROCK!

He is the Rock. His work is perfect.
Deuteronomy 32:4a (LB)

Today's Truth:
Jesus is my refuge;
my protector always.

Rock:
strong person – acting
as a support, refuge, or
defense

Prayer of Praise

Yes, my life is firmly planted on the Rock, Christ Jesus! You are stronger than any circumstance in my life! I praise You for being my support in my time of trouble. I praise You because You are a shield— a defense before and around me. As I trust in You today, I can depend absolutely on You to be that strong, solid Person in my life! Hallelujah! Amen.

Personal Meditation

Day 36

...You are faithful.

Everything He does is just and fair. He is faithful, without sin.
Deuteronomy 32:4b (LB)

Today's Truth:
I can always depend on my
Heavenly Father.

Faithful:

unwavering
reliable
constant

Prayer of Praise

To think of how consistent and available You are, Father God, helps
me to know that I can always reach You! Praise be to You for loving
me as much as any other child in Your family. I give You my deep
appreciation and praise for always having time to listen to me, for
caring about the minute details of my life, and for Your continuing
grace and mercy. Amen.

Personal Meditation

Day 37

...You are my judge and defender.

May the LORD be our judge and decide between us.
May he consider my cause and uphold it; may he vindicate me
by delivering me from your hand.
1 Samuel 24:15 (NIV)

Today's Truth:
The Lord Himself stands
at the gate of my heart
and my life.

Prayer of Praise

Lord Jesus, thank You for representing me perfectly to the Father. I know He sees me through Your eyes and with Your heart. To realize also that You defend me against my enemy, Satan, is awesome. You, Jesus, defeated him by not only dying for my sins, but rising from the dead. You shield me from Satan's attacks and always support and protect me. Hallelujah, You are my Savior! Amen.

Personal Meditation

Day 38

...You are my shield and my helper.

What blessings are yours, O Israel! Who else has been saved by the Lord?
He is your shield and your helper! He is your excellent sword!
Deuteronomy 33:29a (LB)

Today's Truth:
In the Lord Jesus Christ
I am secure.

Shield:

protection
defense
armor
security

Prayer of Praise

Father, You are a shield about me, above me and beneath me. What marvelous protection You provide. You are my safeguard from Satan, the world and even myself. Everyone else may let me down and, at times, even forsake me. In my need, You provide Your peace, relief, a quiet spirit, and even joy! You are my guard and escort! Amen.

Personal Meditation

Day 39

...You, Jehovah, are the mighty God.

For the LORD your God dried up the Jordan before you until you had crossed over...He did this so that all the peoples of the earth might know that the hand of the LORD is powerful and so that you might always fear the LORD your God.
Joshua 4:23a, 24 (NIV)

Today's Truth:
The hand of God is powerful! Always!

Mighty:
powerful
invincible

Prayer of Praise

Father, what a sight it must have been to see the waters of the Jordan River piled high on both sides! Not only that, but a dry path to walk through from one side to the other! Incredible! Fantastic! Humanly impossible! Only You, God... only You!! These mighty acts make it even easier for me to praise such a powerful and strong God... and to entrust my life to Your care. Amen.

Personal Meditation

Day 40

...You are the Promise-Keeper.

*And now, LORD God, keep forever the promise you have made
concerning your servant and his house. Do as you promised,
so that your name will be great forever.*
2 Samuel 7:25-26a (NIV)

Today's Truth:
God's Word is absolutely
trustworthy.

Promise:

agreement
pledge

Prayer of Praise

O Father, how comforting to know that You do keep every promise You
have spoken in Your Word!
Every promise is mine:
> the promise of salvation,
> the promise to reveal Yourself when I seek You wholeheartedly,
> the promise that Your children will never be out of Your sight.
Oh so many promises that on this side of Jordan, I can't possibly know
them all! I praise You because You keep Your Word. Amen.

Personal Meditation

Day 41

...I can trust what You say.

O Sovereign LORD, you are God! Your words are
trustworthy, and you have promised these good things
to your servant.
2 Samuel 7:28 (NIV)

Today's Truth:
God's Word and counsel
is true.

Trustworthy:
reliable, certain
true
unfailing, accurate

Prayer of Praise

Father, it is wonderful to realize that the Bible is filled with truth, because You are Truth. As I put on the piece of armor called "the belt of truth," I realize that Your Word is the glue in my life that holds everything else in place. To know that You are absolutely trustworthy and reliable brings deep peace to my soul. Amen.

Personal Meditation

...You show Your perfection and purity to your children.

To the faithful you show yourself faithful,
to the blameless you show yourself blameless,
to the pure you show yourself pure,
but to the crooked you show yourself shrewd.
2 Samuel 22:26-27 (NIV)

Today's Truth:
In Christ I find my righteousness.

Pure:
uncorrupted
spotless

Prayer of Praise

Father, to realize I stand faultless before You is an absolute marvel to me! I praise You, Jesus, for making this possible by clothing me in Your righteousness. You alone are the genuine God... there is no other. The knowledge that nothing can defile You takes my breath away, because I live in this world so scarred by sin. I praise You for choosing to look at me through the blamelessness of Jesus Christ. Amen.

Personal Meditation

Day 43

...You keep me from harm.

You will save those in trouble,
but you bring down the haughty;
for you watch their every move.
2 Samuel 22:28 (LB)

Today's Truth:

My God preserves me
in times of trouble.

Trouble:

affliction
heartache
danger
difficulty

Prayer of Praise

O Father, You are good... You are righteous... You are right! Hallelujah,
what a Savior... no wonder I praise You. When I am afflicted and in
trouble, You rescue me. From my sin, You rescued me. When I was in
despair, You rescued me. When my loss was more than I could bear,
You touched my heart. How can I do less than give You all praise and
honor and glory. Amen.

Personal Meditation

Day 44

...The paths You choose are perfect.

As for God, his way is perfect; the word of the LORD is flawless...
2 Samuel 22:31a (NIV)

Today's Truth:
God's way is the best way.

Perfect:

faultless
beyond compare
without error or blemish

Prayer of Praise

Father, in a world where "perfect" is hard to come by, I praise You for being flawless in thought, word, and deed. I find such peace in knowing You set before me a chosen pathway. Help and guide me daily to be like You, Jesus – in my thoughts, in my words and in what I do. Amen.

Personal Meditation

Day 45

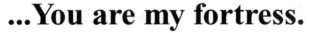

...You are my fortress.

He shields all who hide behind him.
Our Lord alone is God;
We have no other Savior.
God is my strong fortress;
He has made me safe.
He causes the good to walk a steady tread
like mountain goats upon the rocks.
2 Samuel 22:31b-34 (LB)

Today's Truth:
I need no other savior.

Fortress:
stronghold
defense

Prayer of Praise

You are my hiding place, my high tower, the One to Whom I can run and find rest. O Father, so often You have kept me on a steady course. When I began to slip, and knew I could not go on, You carried me and placed my feet with Yours. Yes, You are indeed a shield, a haven. When I come to You, I find myself becoming stronger and able to go on in peace. I praise Your holy name. Amen.

Personal Meditation

Day 46

...You give me strength for daily battles.

*This is what the LORD says to you: "Do not be afraid
or discouraged because of this vast army.
For the battle is not yours, but God's."
2 Chronicles 20:15b (NIV)*

Today's Truth:
God has claimed all my
struggles as His own.

Battle:

conflict
attack
struggle

Prayer of Praise

Each day has its own conflicts, Father, and I praise You because in the
midst of them, You not only give me strength, but remind me that You
are out in front, claiming the battle as Your own. I will not stumble
or fall with You as my Lord. Thank You for guiding me each day onto
Your path, which is truth and peace. Amen.

Personal Meditation

...You raise up leaders to rescue Your people.

*So the Lord raised up leaders among the Israelis to rescue them
from the tyranny of the Syrians; and then Israel lived
in safety again as they had in former days.*
2 Kings 13:5 (LB)

Today's Truth:
The Good Shepherd,
our Lord, will lead us to
safety.

Leader:

guide
ruler
shepherd

Prayer of Praise

Father, You are alive! You see my need, hear my cry, and rescue me!
One day I shall stand in Your presence and heaven will be my new
home—with You, my almighty Leader. Thank You for raising up
leaders to fulfill Your purposes. I praise You for giving us godly men
and women who lead us with truth and righteousness. Amen.

Personal Meditation

Day 48

...You alone are the God of all the kingdoms of the earth.

And Hezekiah prayed to the LORD: "O LORD, God of Israel, enthroned between the cherubim, you alone are God over all the kingdoms of the earth. You have made heaven and earth."
2 Kings 19:15 (NIV)

Today's Truth:
God rules over all… forever.

Kingdoms:
domain
monarchy
realm
empire

Prayer of Praise

To realize that You rule all the kingdoms of the world and see them separately and yet all at once is AMAZING! What a day that will be, Father, when every knee bows and every tongue confesses that You are God: the God of the mighty and the meek; the God of the rich and the poor; the God of all skin colors; the God of the believer and the unbeliever. Your dominion is forever and Your Word is the last word. Amen.

Personal Meditation

...You are the only real God, the only One capable of creation!

For all the gods of the nations are idols, but the LORD made the heavens.
1 Chronicles 16:26 (NIV)

Today's Truth:
My Lord is Master Creator.

gods:
false deities
idols

Prayer of Praise

As I look into the heavens and see the moon and stars at night and the sun by day, I praise You because You are the creator of it all. Yet Your Word tells me that I have not seen anything yet! What You are preparing for Your children when we get to heaven is more than we can even imagine. Only You, Lord, can do such great and marvelous things. I stand in quiet awe today. Amen.

Personal Meditation

...You see every heart and understand and know every thought.

Solomon, my son, get to know the God of your fathers. Worship and serve him with a clean heart and a willing mind, for the Lord sees every heart and understands and knows every thought. If you seek him, you will find him; but if you forsake him, he will permanently throw you aside.
1 Chronicles 28:9 (LB)

Today's Truth:
He knows and understands me
like no other.

Understand:
penetrate
discern
perceive

Prayer of Praise

Oh how I praise You... how can my words express my heart? I praise You for understanding my thoughts even when my words are inadequate. I praise You, Father, for how deeply You know me, and for making Yourself available to be known – if I am just willing to seek You with all my heart. To be known by You... and to have the privilege of knowing You – no earthly riches can compare to these! Amen.

Personal Meditation

Day 51

...You are the Master of all.

*Yours, O LORD, is the greatness and the power and the glory
and the majesty and the splendor, for everything in heaven
and earth is yours. Yours, O LORD is the kingdom;
you are exalted as head over all.*
1 Chronicles 29:11 (NIV)

Today's Truth:
God is my captain and my
Lord; I belong to Him.

Head:

master
captain
director

Prayer of Praise

You spoke, and it was! The elephant, the sun, even the pesky mosquito… it's all Yours. It belongs to You, the Master, Maker, and Director. I praise You for giving me the privilege to know You as Father and to be a precious child of Your kingdom. I ask You now to be the master of my heart and my life today and every day. Amen.

Personal Meditation

...You rule and control everything.

Riches and honor come from you alone, and you are the Ruler of all mankind; your hand controls power and might, and it is at your discretion that men are made great and given strength.
1 Chronicles 29:12 (LB)

Today's Truth:

My God lifts me up and gives strength for the moment.

Rule:

govern
control
manage
order

Prayer of Praise

Before this day began, You knew every need I would have and You had already made provisions for each one. My praises seem so inadequate. Still, I offer You praise for the loving and careful way You manage everything! Some days, dear Father, it seems that my life is out of control! Hallelujah, with You, that NEVER happens! So I rest in You, Father, Who are always in control and Who always keeps my best interests in mind. Amen.

Personal Meditation

...You hear the prayers of Your people.

...if my people, who are called by my name, will humble themselves and pray and seek my face and turn from their wicked ways, then will I hear from heaven and will forgive their sin and will heal their land.
2 Chronicles 7:14 (NIV)

Today's Truth:

As I submit unto God and sincerely seek Him – He brings healing!

Pray:

ask
appeal
beseech
implore

Prayer of Praise

In giving Your Son as the sacrifice for my sin, You made a way for me to come close to You. You ask that I submit, pray, seek, and turn from my wicked selfishness. When I do, You promise to hear, forgive, and heal. May my life always reflect Your integrity so others, too, will be drawn to You. Amen.

Personal Meditation

Day 54

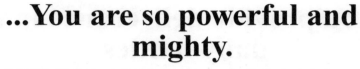

...You are so powerful and mighty.

O LORD, God of our fathers, are you not the God who is in heaven?
You rule over all the kingdoms of the nations. Power and might are in
your hand, and no one can withstand you.
2 Chronicles 20:6 (NIV)

Today's Truth:
In every situation, my Lord
prevails.

Withstand:
oppose
face
defy
confront

Prayer of Praise

When I am afraid or discouraged, I need but stop and pray, because...
    You never leave me.
    You stand alongside me.
    Nothing is too difficult for You.
    You hear my slightest whisper.
    You are always in charge.
    I am never out of Your sight.
Oh Father, how I lift You up in praise!! Amen.

Personal Meditation

Day 55

...You provide deliverance in my daily battles.

You will not have to fight this battle. Take up your positions; stand firm and see the deliverance the LORD will give you, O Judah and Jerusalem. Do not be afraid; do not be discouraged. Go out to face them tomorrow, and the LORD will be with you.
2 Chronicles 20:17 (NIV)

Today's Truth:
God asks that I stand – but He will deliver.

Deliverance:
liberation
salvation
rescue

Prayer of Praise

I stand quietly in Your presence, praising You for delivering me from sin, hell, the power of death, and Satan. No one but You, Jesus, could redeem me. As I live today, I praise You because nothing can confront me that You have not examined and allowed for a purpose. What a mighty God I serve! Amen.

Personal Meditation

...You are awesome yet personal.

*"O Lord God," I cried out; "O great and awesome God
who keeps his promises and is so loving and kind to those
who love and obey him! Hear my prayer!"*
Nehemiah 1:5 (LB)

Today's Truth:
God's great lovingkindness is
sure for those who love and
obey Him.

Awesome:
awe-inspiring
magnificent
great
lofty

Prayer of Praise

Father, You are the promise and hope for each tomorrow. You desire
my obedience, yet You remain steadfast in mercy and grace even when
I stumble. I know You hear my every prayer, for You have promised to
never turn Your back on me. I praise You... I thank You... I love You,
Lord. Amen.

Personal Meditation

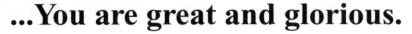

Day 57

...You are great and glorious.

Then as I looked over the situation, I called together the leaders and the people and said to them, "Don't be afraid! Remember the Lord who is great and glorious; fight for your friends, your families, and your homes!"
Nehemiah 4:14 (LB)

Today's Truth:
In the Lord, I have nothing to fear.

Glorious:
exalted
honored
splendid
radiant

Prayer of Praise

Father, I praise You because when I am obedient to You, You frustrate the plans of Satan in my life. I know that in choosing the way of the Lord, I allow You freedom to war on my behalf. I exchange my will for Yours, Lord Jesus. Open my mind that it may be aligned with Yours. I wish to love and obey You. I desire to daily see how great and glorious You are in my life. Amen.

Personal Meditation

Day 58

...Your miraculous acts are beyond comprehension.

He performs wonders that cannot be fathomed,
miracles that cannot be counted.
Job 5:9 (NIV)

Today's Truth:
My God works wonders!

Miracle:

supernatural event
marvelous wonder

Prayer of Praise

Father, only when I get to heaven will I fully know and appreciate all the miracles You have performed in my life. Today I praise You for:
    the miracle of human life,
    the miracle of my salvation,
    the miracle of the body of Christ around the world,
    the miracle of day following night and night following day.
It is so true that Your miracles are marvelous and without number.
Amen.

Personal Meditation

_____
_____
_____
_____
_____
_____

Day 59

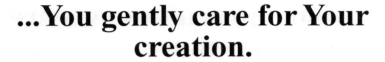

...You gently care for Your creation.

*He sends the rain upon the earth to water the fields, and gives prosperity
to the poor and humble, and takes sufferers to safety.*
Job 5:10-11 (LB)

Today's Truth:
I need not be discouraged;
God cares for me.

Prosperity:

success
favor
abundance

Prayer of Praise

Nothing is too difficult for You! There is nothing that Your hand cannot
do and nothing that Your eye does not see! Even those who mourn
and those who are hungry are never out of Your sight. The grass, the
trees, the flowers of the field... all are nourished and sustained by You,
Heavenly Father. I worship and praise You today. Amen.

Personal Meditation

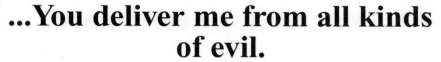

Day 60

...You deliver me from all kinds of evil.

He will deliver you again and again, so that no evil can touch you.
Job 5:19 (LB)
You will be safe from slander; no need to fear the future.
Job 5:21 (LB)

Today's Truth:
I have no need to fear the words of others.

Slander:
misrepresentation which injures a reputation

Prayer of Praise

You deliver me and support me, Father. Every day Your children are exposed to things that are unwholesome and harmful. But hallelujah! You protect me again and again! Only when I get to heaven will I know all the ways You have gone before me... Your watchcare keeps me from being anxious and afraid. Amen.

Personal Meditation

Day 61

...You are my inheritance.

*The Lord himself is my inheritance, my prize. He is my food
and drink, my highest joy! He guards all that is mine.
Psalm 16:5 (LB)*

Today's Truth:

The Lord is my sustenance
and the greatest joy of my life.

inheritance:

gift
gain
legacy
heritage

Prayer of Praise

Father, I need no other like I need You. Your Word says so clearly that
You are my spiritual food and drink. No one could bring me more
lasting joy. You protect all that belongs to me. What a marvelous
inheritance I have in You! Amen.

Personal Meditation

...You, Lord, are a just and mighty God.

If it is a matter of strength, he is mighty! And if it is a matter of justice, who will summon him?
Job 9:19 (NIV)

Today's Truth:

There is no greater strength or justice beyond that which characterizes my Lord!

Summon:

order to appear

Prayer of Praise

You, Almighty Father, are the only One able to make all things in my life complete. You are never weak or faltering. Rather, You move with great force and lack nothing. All the injustices of life find reconciliation at Your hand. I praise You that You have reserved for Yourself the role of eternal judge. Amen.

Personal Meditation

Day 63

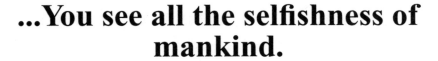

...You see all the selfishness of mankind.

For he knows perfectly all the faults and sins of
mankind; he sees all sin without searching.
Job 11:11 (LB)

Today's Truth:
God knows my faults.

Faults:

defects
shortcomings
weaknesses

Prayer of Praise

Lord, nothing slips by You unnoticed. You know my heart, my thoughts, my motives… You know all my faults and the selfishness I would so like to hide, and yet You love me anyway! How comforting that Your love is not based on my performance! Great are You, Lord, the One Who holds onto me. Amen.

Personal Meditation

Day 64

...You are supremely wise and understanding.

*To God belong wisdom and power; counsel and
understanding are his.*
Job 12:13 (NIV)

Today's Truth:
God is my most capable
counselor.

Wisdom:
discernment
insight

Prayer of Praise

Father, it seems that every day nations are coming against nations in
efforts to control and dominate. I praise You that You alone make sound
judgements that are based on truth and discernment. You alone have
ultimate strength and the capacity for exercising perfect control. I rest
in You today, because as certain as the sun comes up, You will lead me
in what I should and should not do. Amen.

Personal Meditation

Day 65

...Your might is great!

And how great is his might! What he destroys can't be rebuilt.
When he closes in on a man, there is no escape.
Job 12:14 (LB)

Today's Truth:
God is completely sovereign.
He exercises absolute judgment
and authority.

Destroy:

utterly ruin

Prayer of Praise

Father, as I read Your Word, I realize that there are places... like Jericho, Sodom, Gomorrah... that You utterly destroyed and mankind has never rebuilt. I am reminded today that what You put to an end remains that way. Though it is hard for me to think of Your dreadful power, I know this, too, is a part of Your character. I find peace, Father, and praise You for the fact that in Your might You are also perfectly just. Amen.

Personal Meditation

Day 66

...You bring structure to the universe.

Dominion and awe belong to God; he establishes
order in the heights of heaven.
Job 25:2 (NIV)

Today's Truth:
God has a pattern for all things,
great and small.

Order:

organization
structure
harmony

Prayer of Praise

You are splendid, Father, in all Your glory. Even the stars and moon
that You created are less than nothing compared to You. I can only
imagine what it was like the moment You spoke and the moon came
to be; when You spoke and all the galaxies of stars were formed and
took their places in the heavens. You have given each star a name; yet
You shine brighter and fairer than all that You have created. I choose to
praise You, Father... You are beyond description. Amen.

Personal Meditation

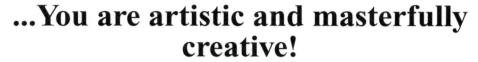

Day 67

...You are artistic and masterfully creative!

He spreads out the northern skies over empty space; he suspends the earth over nothing. He wraps up the waters in his clouds, yet the clouds do not burst under their weight.
Job 26:7-8 (NIV)

Today's Truth:
God can put something beautiful in place of something empty.

Suspends:
hangs freely

Prayer of Praise

Father, You have created the earth to be my home. Indeed, it is filled with wonder. How do You do all these incredible things? You stretch out heaven over empty space. You hang the earth on nothing. You made clouds that hold rain without splitting or bursting. Oh how I praise You, my Creator and Sustainer. Amen.

Personal Meditation

Day 68

...You determine the edges of life itself.

He sets a boundary for the ocean, yes, and a boundary for the day and for the night.
Job 26:10 (LB)

Today's Truth:

God alone will determine the beginning and end of all things.

Boundary:

limit
barrier
border
frame

Prayer of Praise

Father, I stood at the ocean's edge and marveled that it could go only as far inland as its boundary allowed. You set its limit and confined it to a certain end – that You designed. These boundaries give order to our world. As part of Your creation, Lord, we benefit from the boundaries You set out for us in Your Word. Amen.

Personal Meditation

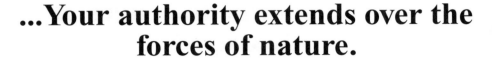

Day 69

...Your authority extends over the forces of nature.

And by his power the sea grows calm; he is skilled at crushing its pride!
Job 26:12 (LB)

Today's Truth:
Even Nature must obey my
Lord.

Power:
force
muscle
strength

Prayer of Praise

Father, I praise You today because You never lack the ability to act with strength or force. Nothing You have created is outside the realm of Your control. What a realization... You do all this and positively never do it for evil or wrong. How wonderful to come to You today and rest in Your perfect management of the universe. Amen.

Personal Meditation

Day 70

...You are above all things and yet do not despise us.

God is mighty, but does not despise men; he is mighty, and firm in his purpose.
Job 36:5 (NIV)

Today's Truth:
God, who is all-powerful, loves the weak, and does not reject anyone who comes to Him with humility.

Despise:
reject

Prayer of Praise

Father, You alone deserve my worship and my complete obedience. You humbled Yourself and became like me to save me. You made it all about me when it is really all about You. Why You consider me and have crowned me with glory I do not understand or fathom. You do not despise that which is under You. You demonstrate Your love toward us by exalting us into the heavenly places with You. I praise Your name. I will learn to gaze upon You. Amen.

Personal Meditation

Day 71

...You are the ultimate teacher.

God is exalted in his power. Who is a teacher like him?
Job 36:22 (NIV)

Today's Truth:
God is my most excellent teacher.

Teacher:
instructor
trainer

Prayer of Praise

Complete... thoroughly qualified... informed... exact... correct...
Father, all these words describe You perfectly in Your ability to
think, retain knowledge, and communicate Your truth to us. You are
unequalled! Therefore, I submit myself to You as Your student...Teach
me Your ways always and I will walk in them. Show me Your paths
that I might set my face like flint. Give me an undivided heart in
seeking out Your truth. What a Savior I have... what a Savior I love.
Amen.

Personal Meditation

Day 72

...Your wonderful works are beyond comprehension!

*God's voice thunders in marvelous ways; he does
great things beyond our understanding.*
Job 37:5 (NIV)

Today's Truth:
God's ways are wonderful and
beyond our comprehension.

Marvelous:

miraculous
wonderful

Prayer of Praise

How great! How awesome You are, God! In all Your ways You teach
me to walk, and yet how unfathomable they are to search out. When
You speak, it is with authority and complete understanding; therefore
I place my trust in You to guide me today. Your voice is peace to my
soul, and in You I rest. Amen.

Personal Meditation

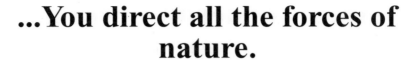

...You direct all the forces of nature.

*He says to the snow, "Fall on the earth," and to the rain shower,
"Be a mighty downpour."
Job 37:6 (NIV)
The breath of God produces ice, and the broad waters become frozen.
Job 37:10 (NIV)*

Today's Truth:
God is in complete control over
all of creation.

Direct:
control
guide

Prayer of Praise

At times, Lord, I sense my heart is like the rain...just wanting to pour myself out; or that my life is like a raging storm. As I consider these times in my life, I am reminded of Your hand stretching out over the waters and Your voice speaking "Peace. Be still. Know that I am God." You are God. Oh, that You would speak to my heart and cause me to know that You are my God, and that You are in complete control. Amen.

Personal Meditation

...Even nature fulfills Your purposes.

He loads the clouds with moisture and they send forth his lightning. The lightning bolts are directed by his hand, and do whatever he commands throughout the earth. He sends the storms as punishment, or, in his lovingkindness, to encourage.
Job 37:11-13 (LB)

Today's Truth:
God's character, judgements and loving-kindness are displayed in the natural elements.

Encourage:
uplift
inspire

Prayer of Praise

Your creation describes You in so many ways...the thunder–Your power and might; the lightning–Your pervasive response; the rain–Your gentle mercies which are new every morning. I sometimes find myself absorbed in my circumstances and only look inside me. And then You lift my face and cause me to behold Your handiwork; the workings of Your heavens and all their glory. You remind me that it's not what comes my way, but how I respond to it. The weather reveals that Your intimate touch is so often needed in the circumstances in my life. Therefore, mold me Lord! Cause patience to have its perfect work in me, that I might be perfect and complete, lacking nothing. Amen.

Personal Meditation

Day 75

...You watch over everything that concerns me.

*For the Lord watches over all the plans and paths of godly
men, but the paths of the godless lead to doom.*
Psalm 1:6 (LB)

Today's Truth:
God guides the paths of those
who love Him.

Godly:

filled with love for God

Prayer of Praise

Before I opened my eyes this morning, Father, You had already set my
day in motion. You had prepared my steps and knew all my plans and
the paths they would lead me down. It places me at rest when I put my
confidence in You. I praise You because You are always attentive to my
needs. When I cry out to you, You are already there...hearing, feeling,
and answering. I cannot help but praise a God like You. Amen.

Personal Meditation

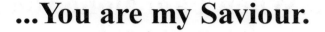

Day 76

...You are my Saviour.

For salvation comes from God. What joys he
gives to all his people.
Psalm 3:8 (LB)

Today's Truth:
The Lord is the great deliverer.

Salvation:
freedom
deliverance

Prayer of Praise

Father, I marvel at the fact that through Christ's work on the cross I am delivered from sin, hell, and Satan. Through Your own sacrifice you made a way for me to be reconciled to You. You have bestowed Your glory upon me and have now become my Hope. My salvation brings me such great joy! For as Your child, I belong to Your family forever. Thank You. Amen.

Personal Meditation

Day 77

...When I am alone You keep me safe.

I will lie down in peace and sleep, for though I am
alone, O Lord, you will keep me safe.
Psalm 4:8 (LB)

Today's Truth:
God is my safety.

Safe:

secure

unharmed

Prayer of Praise

When I consider Your presence, Father, I think of safety and security. You have said that You will never leave me or forsake me, and that You are a hedge to me on my right and on my left. Sometimes You draw others away from me and allow me to feel alone that I might learn to lean on You more. And yet in this I am confident, that even in my darkest nights I am not alone. I have put my trust in You. Even when I lie down to sleep, I will do so in peace because You never sleep! I am secure and protected in the palm of Your hand. Amen.

Personal Meditation

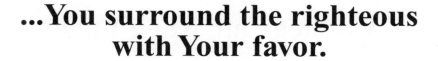

Day 78

...You surround the righteous with Your favor.

For surely, O LORD, you bless the righteous;
you surround them with your favor as with a shield.
Psalm 5:12 (NIV)

Today's Truth:
God's favor is upon the righteous.

Surround:

envelope
enclose

Prayer of Praise

I cannot begin to count all the ways Your blessings surround me, Father. You have given me every spiritual blessing, and every good gift has been from You. You have granted me eternal life, Your Holy Spirit, and Your precious Word. You bring Christian brothers and sisters alongside me to encourage and lift me up. You have given me a heart to understand Your truth and to be obedient to Your commandments. You have provided tools for me to communicate Your love and compasson to others. I lift my hands and stand in awe of You, Lord. You have met my every need. Your grace has been more than enough. I bless Your name. Amen.

Personal Meditation

...You hear me when I pray.

The LORD has heard my cry for mercy;
the LORD accepts my prayer.
Psalm 6:9 (NIV)

Today's Truth:

God hears those who cry out
to Him.

Hear:

give attention
heed

Prayer of Praise

As I walk in righteousness and integrity, I know that You hear my
prayers. I sit quietly in Your presence, Father, knowing that You listen
to my heart. My fears and needs today will not go unnoticed by You.
I praise You for extending to me Your mercy. Your arm has not been
shortened nor has Your ear grown hard of hearing, but You are ready
and willing to answer all who call upon Your name. Amen.

Personal Meditation

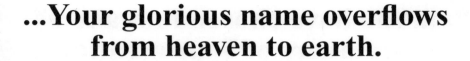

Day 80

...Your glorious name overflows from heaven to earth.

O LORD OUR God, the majesty and glory of your name fills all the earth and overflows the heavens.
Psalm 8:1 (LB)

Today's Truth:
God's glory fills the heavens
and the earth

Majesty:
splendor
renown

Prayer of Praise

Father, I know that at this moment angels surround You, giving You praise and glorifying Your name. It seems amazing to me how vast Your glory is; that even here on earth where I live, I will see Your glory and know the greatness of Your name. For Your fame...Your renown is something that will never pass away. It is unending. Your glory shall cover the earth as water does the sea, and all will know how great a God You are. Amen.

Personal Meditation

Day 81

...You have chosen to make us caretakers of Your creation.

You have put him in charge of everything you made;
everything is put under his authority: all sheep and oxen, and
wild animals too, the birds and fish, and all the life in the sea.
Psalm 8:6-8 (LB)

Today's Truth:
God has placed all of His creation under
the stewardship of mankind.

Caretaker:
servant
steward

Prayer of Praise

Father, You have placed us in charge of all that surrounds us. This is an amazing privilege, yet it comes with great responsibility. Help me to be accountable to You in handling Your creation; that with wisdom and care, I might accomplish all that You've placed under my hand. Help me to be dependable in all my daily tasks that I might someday join the faithful who have preceded me in doing Your will. Amen.

Personal Meditation

...with justice You judge all the nations of the earth.

He will judge the world in righteousness; he
will govern the peoples with justice.
Psalm 9:8 (NIV)

Today's Truth:
God is a just judge.

Justly:
impartially
accurately

Prayer of Praise

The media is filled with news of terrorists, murderers, thieves, abusers, liars...so much darkness and evil! Yet I know that You see it, Lord, and comprehend it all. So I need not seek revenge for wrongs committed against me; I need not be filled with bitterness or despair, for You will fairly judge individuals and nations alike, and the wicked will receive the consequences You deem appropriate. Yet teach me, Lord, to love my enemies. Show me today how I can bless someone who hates me or is spiteful against me, that they may see Your love in me and glorify Your name. Amen.

Personal Meditation

Day 83

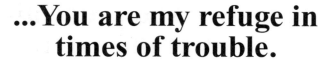

...You are my refuge in times of trouble.

All who are oppressed may come to him. He is a
refuge for them in their times of trouble.
Psalm 9:9 (LB)

Today's Truth:
God is a shelter to the oppressed.

Refuge:
protection
shelter

Prayer of Praise

What a shelter You are for me in times of distress. In my world it is easy to be neglected or overlooked, but You never take your eye from me. When the pressures of my job, family, and other weekly activities come crushing in on me, I run to Your presence to find focus and comfort; Your comfort, Lord, surpasses that of any human concern. When I pass through the waters, I know that You will be with me and shall not allow them to overflow me. You hold my head up. I will rest in You. Amen.

Personal Meditation

...You show Your face to the godly.

For God is good, and he loves goodness;
the godly shall see his face.
Psalm 11:7 (LB)

Today's Truth:

God loves goodness, and desires to
show more of Himself to those who
love goodness too.

Goodness:
excellence
virtue

Prayer of Praise

Moses asked to see Your glory, Lord, even after You had spoken
with him face to face. Those who love You, love Your ways and
come to crave You more and more. They desire to go deeper in their
relationship with You. Father, my prayer to You today is...show me
Your glory! Cause Your goodness to pass before my eyes! For I desire
greater revelation of You. Wherever I am today, draw me into Your
presence and set my focus on what pleases You. I love You. Amen.

Personal Meditation

Day 85

...You add meaning to my life.

I said to the LORD, 'You are my Lord;
apart from you I have no good thing.
Psalm 16:2 (NIV)

Today's Truth:
Nothing that I have outside of
God is good.

Apart:
separated
disconnected

Prayer of Praise

You, Father, are above all things that I value. You I esteem; You I honor.
You are the spiritual food and drink for my soul. You are superior in
Your character and are the chief influence in my life. My heart is glad
and my lips will tell others about the joy You put into my life. Because
You are my highest joy, no matter what this day brings, I will rest
securely in the joy of Your presence. Amen.

Personal Meditation

...You provide a rich legacy for Your children.

The boundary lines have fallen for me in pleasant places; surely I have a delightful inheritance.
Psalm 16:6 (NIV)

Today's Truth:
God's inheritance for His
children is good.

Inheritance:
legacy
heritage

Prayer of Praise

Father, I was lost in darkness. I had gone my own way and stood condemned in my sins. But You searched for me and found me. You redeemed me with a great price; and now you are mine and I am Yours. You have made those who love You Your inheritance, and have given them eternal life. I would rather be a doorkeeper for a day in the house of my God than spend a thousand years elsewhere. In Your presence is fullness of joy, and at Your right hand are pleasures forevermore. Amen.

Personal Meditation

Day 87

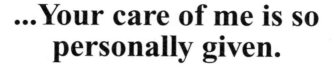

...Your care of me is so personally given.

*Protect me as you would the pupil of your eye; hide me
in the shadow of your wings as you hover over me.*
Psalm 17:8 (LB)

Today's Truth:
God's presence protects me.

Shadow:
covering
protection

Prayer of Praise

Today, Father, I give praise to a God who is so personal. You have
searched me and known me, and understood my most anxious
thoughts. You have hidden me from my enemies and from the evil one.
You have given me the sure mercies of David: the promise of life to
those who delight themselves in You. Your arm has outstretched over
me and I have found rest under the shadow of the Almighty. Amen.

Personal Meditation

Day 88

...You are my stronghold.

The LORD is my rock, my fortress and my deliverer;
my God is my rock, in whom I take refuge. He is my
shield and the horn of my salvation, my stronghold.
Psalm 18:2 (NIV)

Today's Truth:
God is a fortress to those who
take refuge in Him.

Fortress:
place of safety
stronghold

Prayer of Praise

A place of security... my tower in strength... my defense... Oh Father, I
praise You for letting nothing through to my life that has not first gone
through You! Your protection of me extends to heights my mind and
my eyes cannot begin to take in! You are always armed and equipped
to come against the attacks of the enemy of my soul. You are more
powerful than the mightiest of the mighty, You are my refuge. I will
never be put to shame, because Your walls cannot be broken through.
Amen.

Personal Meditation

Day 89

...There is brilliance in Your presence. You are the One Who gives commands.

Out of the brightness of his presence clouds advanced,
with hailstones and bolts of lightning.
Psalm 18:12 (NIV)

The valleys of the sea were exposed and the foundations of the earth laid
bare at your rebuke, O LORD, at the blast of breath from your nostrils.
Psalm 18:15 (NIV)

Rebuke:
strong disapproval

Prayer of Praise

Father, this verse has come alive to me. I have recently watched as killer waves seemingly came out of nowhere to take lives, homes, livelihoods; and in a few moments, the foundations of the earth were laid bare. I have wept over the great loss of lives, but I am keenly made aware that You are still in control of all things. Amen.

Personal Meditation

...All Your ways are perfect.

What a God he is! How perfect in every way!
All his promises prove true. He is a shield for
everyone who hides behind him.
Psalm 18:30-31 (LB)

Today's Truth:
God's ways and methods are
excellent.

Perfect:
excellent
complete

Prayer of Praise

There is such peace for me, Father, to know that You are always
correct, exact, and accurate in all Your ways. Your words never return
to You unfulfilled, but accomplish the purposes for which You speak
them—Your promises never fail. Your methods are designed for every
circumstance so that You might gain utmost glory, and that Your
name might be exalted above all worldly wisdom. Therefore, I have
believed in You, and I am persuaded, that You are able and faithful to
keep all that I've committed to You until that final day. Amen.

Personal Meditation

Day 91

...You are the living God.

The LORD lives! Praise be to my Rock! Exalted be God my Savior.
Psalm 18:46 (NIV)

Today's Truth:
God is alive. He hears our prayers of praise and gives us strength.

Live:
abide
dwell
exist

Prayer of Praise

People worldwide worship gods that cannot see or hear or speak. But You, God, are alive! You hear my every prayer, and You give me strength for the difficulties I encounter each day. You prepare me for the conflicts and disputes that I face. I lift my hands to You with thanksgiving and praise in my heart that You are alive and give me strength to face the challenges of each day. Amen.

Personal Meditation

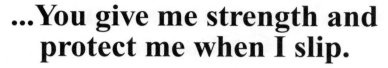

Day 92

...You give me strength and protect me when I slip.

You have made wide steps beneath my feet
so that I need never slip.
Psalm 18:36 (LB)

Today's Truth:
Our God protects and defends
us against evil.

Slip:
lapse
mistake
err

Prayer of Praise

Father, I realize that You defend me from spiritual peril. You are my shield when attacks and harm assail me. The attacks come from Satan, the world, and sometimes from my own choices. Please, Father, keep my feet on the solid ground You have for me and help me to stand firm against temptations that lead me down a slippery, treacherous path away from You. I praise You for Your daily protection. Amen.

Personal Meditation

Day 93

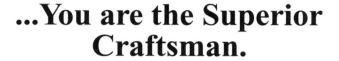

...You are the Superior Craftsman.

The heavens are telling the glory of God; they are a
marvelous display of his craftsmanship.
Psalm 19:1 (LB)

Today's Truth:

God has created the wonders
of our world.

Craftsman:
skilled worker
artisan

Prayer of Praise

God Almighty, You do such great works. It is beyond my ability to comprehend: stars that hang in space, the creation of a baby, seasons that change, the love of a man and woman for each other, frogs and turtles that breathe buried deep in the mud, the unique pattern of each snowflake... Thank You, Father, for blessing me with Your marvelous works! Amen.

Personal Meditation

...You alone rule the nations!

For the Lord is King and rules the nations.
Psalm 22:28 (LB)

Today's Truth:
The Lord is ruler over everything,
including the ordinary events of my
everyday life.

Rule:
reign
govern
order

Prayer of Praise

Father, I need Your strength and support every day. How wonderful to
know that I can always rely on You! You direct my steps and protect
me. Your Word states that even in the course of ordinary events, You
are the authority; You are the one in control. Nations often do not want
to admit that You rule them, but You are King over all. How great is
Your influence! Amen.

Personal Meditation

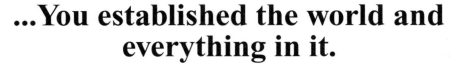

Day 95

...You established the world and everything in it.

The earth is the LORD'S and everything in it, the world, and all who live in it; for he founded it upon the seas and established it upon the waters.
Psalm 24:1-2 (NIV)

Today's Truth:
God created the entire world, all that has existed in the past, what is here now, and what will be in the future.

Establish:
build
root
create

Prayer of Praise

In the world around me, my eyes see and my ears hear Your splendor and magnificence. Everything has its roots in You, Father. I praise You for beautiful sunsets, music, rainbows painted across the sky, a baby's sweet smile and so much more! Thank You for all the past, present, and future blessings of this world. Amen.

Personal Meditation

Day 96

...You are my only hope.

Lead me; teach me; for you are the God who gives
me salvation. I have no hope except in you.
Psalm 25:5 (LB)

Today's Truth:
God leads and teaches us. He
is our hope and salvation.

Hope:
expectation
longing
desire

Prayer of Praise

You are an amazing God, Heavenly Father! Only You, through Your
mercy and grace, can give salvation. With Jesus as my Savior, I have a
future filled with hope and the promise that I will live with You forever.
Your Word teaches, leads and directs my life. I praise You for the hope
that only You can give. Amen.

Personal Meditation

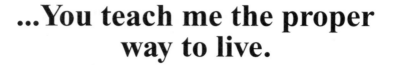

Day 97

...You teach me the proper way to live.

He guides the humble in what is right and teaches them his way.
Psalm 25:9 (NIV)

Today's Truth:
God guides and teaches us
His way.

Teach:
develop
train
nurture

Prayer of Praise

When I am pulled in so many different directions, Father, You are beside me to show me the right way. You not only teach me what is right, but also what is appropriate and proper to say and do in all situations. Humble my heart that my words and actions might lead others to You. Amen.

Personal Meditation

...You are my Friend and You share who You are with me.

Friendship with God is reserved for those who reverence him. With them alone he shares the secrets of his promises.
Psalm 25:14 (LB)

Today's Truth:
God desires friendship with us.
Through our relationship
with Him, He shares His promises.

Friend:
supporter
ally
confidante

Prayer of Praise

It is amazing to me that You desire my friendship. I look upon You with awe and profound respect. I praise You that our friendship is growing as You regularly reveal Yourself to me through Your Word. I praise You for the blessings of our friendship. Amen.

Personal Meditation

...You are my light in a dark world.

The LORD is my light and my salvation—whom
shall I fear? The LORD is the stronghold of my
life—of whom shall I be afraid?
Psalm 27:1 (NIV)

Today's Truth:
The Lord is by my side,
lighting my path, offering
salvation.

Light:
beacon
torch

Prayer of Praise

Lord, I need You to be my light and stronghold now... today!
Everywhere I turn there is sin. What a blessing to know that You are
my light in the darkness that surrounds me. Only You, Father, are able
to save me from sin, Satan, the world… and even my own flesh. I
praise You for being my strength through each day's perils. I praise
You that with You by my side, I need not be afraid. Amen.

Personal Meditation

Day 100

...Your presence in my life gives me confidence to press on.

I am still confident of this: I will see the
goodness of the LORD in the land of the living.
Psalm 27:13 (LB)

Today's Truth:

The Lord is with us. No matter
what challenges we face, we can
be confident that the Lord will
see us through it.

Confident:

secure
certain
assured

Prayer of Praise

Father, I praise You for all the times You have been beside me through
the challenges I have faced. Thank You for helping me to see the
goodness in the world that surrounds me through those people that You
have placed in my life to help me. Amen.

Personal Meditation

...You give me strength for each day.

The LORD is my strength and my shield; my heart
trusts in him, and I am helped. My heart leaps for
joy and I will give thanks to him in song.
Psalm 28:7 (NIV)

Today's Truth:
Our strength and help comes from
the Lord.

Strength:
might
power
energy

Prayer of Praise

You, Father, are my strength. Through Your presence in my life I find
the energy to face each day. When I am vulnerable and exposed, You
are my shield, protecting me from spiritual injury. When I experience
loss, You are my support. You guard my way every day and assist me
in decisions I need to make. Thank You, Father, for listening to my
earnest prayer. Amen.

Personal Meditation

Day 102

...Your creation displays Your power and majesty.

The voice of the Lord echoes from the clouds.
The God of glory thunders through the skies.
So powerful is his voice; so full of majesty.
Psalm 29:3-4 (LB)

Today's Truth:

God's power and majesty are awesome!

Power:
authority
energy
control

Prayer of Praise

All of nature, Father, is in Your control. In the midst of the storm, when the lightning flashes and the thunder claps, I am awed by the tremendous and total power You wield over Your creation. You, though stately and dignified, can make a mighty tree collapse and cause mountains to shake and break apart through the power of Your voice. What a mighty and powerful God You are! Amen.

Personal Meditation

...Your anger is short-lived, but Your kindness lasts forever.

For his anger lasts only a moment, but his favor lasts a lifetime; weeping may remain for a night, but rejoicing comes in the morning.
Psalm 30:5 (NIV)

Today's Truth:

God, as our loving Father, disciplines us in love. His grace lasts throughout our lives and into eternity.

Favor:
kindness
grace
benevolence

Prayer of Praise

Dear Loving Father, sometimes I stray away and act in ways that hurt others and You by my words, my attitude and my actions. Thank You for disciplining me in love. Your rebuke brings me back into the circle of Your endless favor and blessing. You are my support, the One I can rely on. You alone give me a contented spirit and a tranquility that no one else can give, much less sustain. I praise You that Your loving kindness lasts forever! Amen.

Personal Meditation

...You know my heartaches and worries.

*I will be glad and rejoice in your love, for you saw
my affliction and knew the anguish of my soul.*
Psalm 31:7 (NIV)

Today's Truth:
God knows us intimately. He always
listens to our troubles and understands
our challenges.

Anguish:
despair
heartache
sorrow

Prayer of Praise

Father, when I am distressed or worried, I know it will ease my heart
to give my burden to You. Every day you provide the strength I need
to face my challenges. You know me intimately. You are never too
busy to notice me and listen to my deepest thoughts and concerns. You
understand my fears. You care! I look for Your saving help every day
and praise You for Your love. Amen

Personal Meditation

...You have stored up great blessings for Your followers.

Oh, how great is your goodness to those who publicly declare that you will rescue them. For you have stored up great blessings for those who trust and reverence you.
Psalm 31:19 (LB)

Today's Truth:
God delights in giving good things to those who trust in Him.

Blessing:
favor
gain
benefits

Prayer of Praise

In a world filled with gods, You alone are my God. No other god in any form, made by human hands, can show the kindness and give the blessings to me that You bestow each day. I have confidence in You, Lord, and commit my day to Your care. I adore You. I stand in awe of You. I give to You all honor, praise, and respect. You alone are my God. Amen.

Personal Meditation

...Your love is like a protective wall around me.

Praise be to the LORD,
for he showed his wonderful love to me
when I was in a besieged city.
Psalm 31:21 (NIV)

Today's Truth:
God is my defense and safety.

Wall:
enclosure

Prayer of Praise

With You, Lord, I have the power to overcome Satan, hurt, sickness and any form of trouble. I know You are near to me in all my stressful situations. I depend on You to guide me. Jesus, You are the High Tower to which I run. You are a steadfast and trustworthy God! Amen.

Personal Meditation

...I find safe harbor in You.

You are my hiding place; you will protect me from trouble
and surround me with songs of deliverance.
Psalm 32:7 (NIV)

Today's Truth:
God is my sanctuary through all the
storms in life.

Storm:
assault
attack
rough time

Prayer of Praise

Father, I praise You beyond what my words can utter for surrounding
me with Your great protection. I realize today that when temptations
and the circumstances of my life become difficult, I can run to You and
find comfort and practical guidance. Today may bring challenges and
struggles, but PRAISE YOU, JESUS... You will be my hiding place in
the turmoil of life! In the middle of the tempests and trials, You enable
me to sing! Amen.

Personal Meditation

...You are my most trustworthy Advisor.

I will instruct you (says the Lord) and guide you along the best pathway for your life; I will advise you and watch your progress.
Psalm 32:8 (LB)

Today's Truth:
God counsels me and always keeps me in His view.

Instruct:
give direction
guide
train

Prayer of Praise

Unrest... difficult circumstances... distress... worry... You enable me to rise with You above them all! Today as I allow You to order and direct my words and decisions, I invite You to show me the best way. Even though I may walk today through fearful situations, I can lean on You for guidance and know that You will walk with me down the most appropriate path. You alone have the right words and qualities in Your character to accompany me on my journey! Your Word is of eminent worth and deserves my trust! Amen.

Personal Meditation

Day 109

...You love me.

The Lord gazes down upon mankind from heaven where he lives.
He has made their hearts and closely watches everything they do.
Psalm 33:13-15 (LB)

Today's Truth:
I am of infinite worth to God.

Closely:
carefully
mindfully

Prayer of Praise

Right now, this very moment, You are watching over me. That kind of care causes me to sit here quietly in awe of You. I trust You because I know You are a dependable God. I praise You for your detailed interest in my life. Tender love... all around me are expressions of this—a mother nursing her baby, a bird feeding its young, a new shoot out of the ground signaling spring has arrived. All these, and so much more, Father, show how You gently, carefully love us and put Your tender love within us. Amen.

Personal Meditation

...When I wait upon You, I find that You are all I need.

We wait in hope for the LORD; he is our help and our shield.
Psalm 33:20 (NIV)

Today's Truth:
The Lord is faithful to come to my aid, if I will just wait on Him!

Wait:
abide
delay
linger

Prayer of Praise

Father, keep me today from rushing into poor decisions that would cause me to stray from Your hand of protection. Help me instead to abide in You and come to know the choices and direction most pleasing to You. Also, guard my tongue from speaking quick, thoughtless, angry, or judgmental words. Rather, give me the desire and commitment to wait for Your words, seasoned with grace, to flow through me. Amen.

Personal Meditation

Day 111

...You respond to a searching spirit.

I sought the LORD, and he answered me;
he delivered me from all my fears.
Psalm 34:4 (NIV)

Today's Truth:
When I seek the Lord, He allows me to find
Him and be fulfilled.

Sought:
followed
inquired
dug for

Prayer of Praise

Father, today I cry out to You and give You praise because I know
You have released me from the bondage of my selfishness and fears.
Many around me are confined and imprisoned by innumerable fears,
but as I am willing to seek You, You faithfully deliver me from them
all! I praise You for Your kindness and compassion for me. You have
given me abundant mercy. Just as the spring rains come, Your mercy is
showered upon me and washes away my anxious fears. Amen.

Personal Meditation

Day 112

...You guard and rescue me.

*For the eyes of the Lord are intently watching all who live good lives,
and he gives attention when they cry to him.*
Psalm 34:15 (LB)

Today's Truth:
God's ear is open to those who cry
out to Him.

Intently:
keenly
attentively
steadily

Prayer of Praise

Father, You are the Sentry of my soul. I know nothing is beyond Your
loving watchful eyes. Your constant guidance, direction, and attention
give comfort in times of distress. Help me, Lord, to live a life that
honors You–a good life that is in accordance with Your calling. Amen.

Personal Meditation

...You hold onto me when I'm in the depths of despair.

The Lord is close to those whose hearts are breaking; he rescues those who are humbly sorry for their sins.
Psalm 34:18 (LB)

Today's Truth:
God is closest to me in my humility.

Close:
near

Prayer of Praise

In my deep time of need, You are there. I praise You for the times when my heart is broken and You comfort me. Lord, when my heart is broken because of my sinfulness, and I am grieved because of how I have failed You–it is there that I find you closest. Oh God, how You come near in those moments. You are my rescuer and I praise You. Amen.

Personal Meditation

Day 114

...You are the champion of the helpless and the needy.

But I will rejoice in the Lord. He shall rescue me! From the bottom of my heart praise rises to him. Where is his equal in all of heaven and earth? Who else protects the weak and helpless from the strong, and the poor and needy from those who would rob them?
Psalm 35:9-10 (LB)

Today's Truth:
God defends the weak.

Champion:
advocate
defender
hero

Prayer of Praise

Father, I was one that was weak, poor, and needy, but You were there with me. You have always been my protector. In every way You are unequaled. When I search in my time of need, what I find is You. You are sufficient for me. I need no other. In You I am complete. I lift my praises unto You. Amen.

Personal Meditation

...Your love knows no limits or boundaries.

Your steadfast love, O Lord, is as great as all the heavens.
Your faithfulness reaches beyond the clouds.
Psalm 36:5 (LB)

Today's Truth:
God's love will never diminish.

Steadfast:
unfaltering
enduring
abiding

Prayer of Praise

What a wonderful thought, Father, to realize that You take pleasure in me being Your child. AMAZING! You are the Stable One in my life. You are my Rock! When I am distant from You, Your love is never distant from me. You, oh God, cannot love me any more than You do, and You have promised to never love me any less! In this I rejoice. How I love You! Amen.

Personal Meditation

Day 116

... the majesty of Your character grows as I come closer to You.

Your righteousness is like the mighty mountains,
Your justice like the great deep. O LORD, you preserve both man and beast.
Psalm 36:6 (NIV)

Today's Truth:
God becomes more beautiful as I
get to know Him more.

Righteousness:
blamelessness

Prayer of Praise

Oh, how beautiful are the mountains of Your creation. As I view them from a distance, they appear approachable and sublime. But when I am in their midst, I see myself in proper perspective. Their vastness seems unending. So, too, is Your justice and righteousness. As I view Your character from a distance, I know You only in limited form, but as I find myself growing closer to You, the more vast and majestic You become. Lord, You inspire me to know more of You. Amen.

Personal Meditation

…Your love is priceless and eternal.

How priceless is your unfailing love! Both high and low among men find refuge in the shadow of your wings.
Psalm 36:7 (NIV)

Today's Truth:
The need for God's unfailing love is universal.

priceless:
beyond evaluation

Prayer of Praise

How can I adequately praise You for Your immeaurable love for me...
a love that existed before I was born,
a love of sacrifice–You gave Your Son to die for my sins,
a love that is unconditional.
How can a price be placed on such a love? You deserve my complete devotion. Lord, Help me hold nothing back from You. Allow me to find my refuge in Your loving shadow. Amen.

Personal Meditation

Day 118

...You direct my steps as I walk in Your ways.

The steps of good men are directed by the Lord. He delights in each step they take. If they fall it isn't fatal, for the Lord holds them with his hand.
Psalm 37:23-24 (LB)

Today's Truth:
God is delighted by each step I take
with Him.

Fatal:
ruin
disastrous
terminal

Prayer of Praise

As I move into my day, I praise You because You are holding my hand! As I take each step, I place my feet in Your footsteps. I know You will carry me when I grow weary or become discouraged. And if I fall today, I know You will lift me up and restore me. You will never let go of my hand. Amen.

Personal Meditation

Day 119

...You delight in fairness.

For the Lord loves justice and fairness; he will never abandon his people.
They will be kept safe forever; but all who love wickedness shall perish.
Psalm 37:28 (LB)

Today's Truth:
God will not abandon me or leave my
future to chance.

Just:
right
impartial

Prayer of Praise

Fairness and justice You love. God, give me Your eyes that I may be just. Give to me Your heart that I may be fair. In my selfish human ways it is difficult to always seek what is right, but You, oh God, are always and absolutely fair. Help me to more consistently see others through Your eyes. Give me a heart of love and not judgement. I want to bring joy to You in how I treat all people. Amen.

Personal Meditation

...Your miracles are all around me!

O Lord my God, many and many a time you have done great miracles for us, and we are ever in your thoughts. Who else can do such glorious things? No one else can be compared with you. There isn't time to tell of all your wonderful deeds.
Psalm 40:5 (LB)

Today's Truth:
I celebrate Your delightful and distinguished works.

Glorious:
triumphant
superb

Prayer of Praise

There are miracles 'round about me every day, Father, such as...
> the miracle of birth.
> the miracle of the sun rising.
> the miracle of planting a seed and seeing it sprout and grow to become whatever You intended it to be.

BUT the greatest miracle of all is the miracle of salvation and the fact that You have placed Your spirit within me, making me a new creation. Today I am a child of God. By this miracle You have allowed me to one day see Your glorious face, sit in Your presence, and say I love You. Amen.

Personal Meditation

...You help and think about me.

I am poor and needy, yet the Lord is thinking
about me right now! O my God, you are my helper.
Psalm 40:17a (LB)

Today's Truth:
I am so important to the Lord that right
now He is thinking about me. I can trust
Him to help me in all of life's situations.

Helper:
supporter
partner
ally

Prayer of Praise

Father, You are more important than and superior to anyone or
anything... and yet You are thinking about me this very instant.
This awareness leaves me completely humbled. It is beyond my
understanding that You, the Great God of the universe, know my every
need and care for me. I give You my deepest praise and raise high
the name of my Lord Jesus Christ that every day I experience Your
comfort and support in my life. Amen.

Personal Meditation

...Even when things are dark and troubled, God's loving care does not change!

Blessed is he who has regard for the weak; the LORD
delivers him in times of trouble.
Psalm 41:1 (NIV)

Today's Truth:

God cares for the weak, poor and needy.
He blesses those who share His concern.

Regard:

concern
respect
observe

Prayer of Praise

Heavenly Father, You care for the weak, poor and needy. While they may lack in strength, intellect or worldly possessions, they are precious in Your sight. I praise You for the constant and enduring way You care for those the world scorns. Please open my eyes and heart that I might reach out to others. I praise You that I experience the richness of Your blessings when I share Your concern and show kindness, respect, and love in Your name. Amen.

Personal Meditation

...You are Everlasting!

Bless the Lord, the God of Israel, who exists from everlasting ages past—and on into everlasting eternity ahead. Amen and amen!
Psalm 41:13 (LB)

Today's Truth:
God has been with me in the past, He is here today, and He will be with me forever.

Everlasting:
eternal
perpetual
infinite

Prayer of Praise

You, Heavenly Father, are the only thing in my world that is everlasting. My days here are numbered... but when I am home— really home—my days, like Yours, Father, will be ceaseless and unending. Today I take great pleasure in being Your child. As I look back, I see Your presence in my life. You have provided strength for each new day. I trust You to guide me today and every day. I look forward to spending eternity in Your presence. I praise You for being the only constant in my life. I praise You today and forever. Amen.

Personal Meditation

...You are my King.

You are my King and my God. Decree victories for your people.
Psalm 44:4 (LB)

Today's Truth:
God rules victoriously above all others; He is the King of my life.

King:
ruler
monarch
sovereign

Prayer of Praise

You, Father, are the one greatest importance in my life. You alone have the strength and power to overcome any "enemy" that I face. So in great confidence, I place my hand into Yours and grip the hand of my victorious King because I know the outcomes of the battles before me are already determined – the enemy will be vanquished, for the victory belongs to Jesus! I honor and praise You as my King. Amen.

Personal Meditation

...You are my refuge and strength.

God is our refuge and strength, an ever-present help in trouble.
Psalm 46:1 (NIV)

Today's Truth:
God provides me with a safe haven and strength for each day's challenges.

Refuge:
sanctuary
harbor
shelter

Prayer of Praise

Kingdoms crumble, leaders fall, life gives way to death... but You, Lord Jesus, remain a safe harbor. You offer me shelter and a safe place to rest when I am weary from the storms of everyday life that assail me. You have unlimited power and authority beyond my imagination, and yet You provide me with personal strength and support for each day's challenges. I am so glad it is not that You "could be" or "might be," but rather that You are all I need! You are my refuge. You are my strength. Amen.

Personal Meditation

...You are unmoved by turmoil.

*There is a river of joy flowing through the City of our God—the
sacred home of the God above all gods. God himself is living
in that City; therefore it stands unmoved despite the turmoil
everywhere. He will not delay his help.*
Psalm 46:4-5 (LB)

Today's Truth:
God's love is unaffected by the events of
this world. I can trust Him to sustain me!

Unmoved:
firm
unaffected

Prayer of Praise

AIDS, murders, missing children, prisoners of war... Oh Father, the
nations of the world truly are in turmoil. The world has turned its back
on You. I praise You for never turning Your back on us. Your love is
constant and unchanging. I praise You, the Lord God Almighty, for
Your steady presence in my life! Amen.

Personal Meditation

Day 127

...You quiet my mind and heart.

*Stand silent! Know that I am God! I will be
honored by every nation in the world!
Psalm 46:10 (LB)*

Today's Truth:
God commands me to be still
so I may hear His voice calling me.

Still:
calm
serene
quiet

Prayer of Praise

Father, the years seem to be flying by with ever-increasing speed.
More than ever before, my life is busy. Often I become so involved in
day-to-day living that I neglect my relationship with You, Lord. Thank
You for commanding me to be still! Thank You for quieting my mind
and heart to hear Your voice speaking to me as I read Your Word. You
alone are above all and deserve to be honored among all peoples of the
world. Amen.

Personal Meditation

...You are a fortress for your children.

The LORD Almighty is with us;
the God of Jacob is our fortress. Selah.
Psalm 46:11 (NIV)

Today's Truth:

God is my fortress, providing my sure defense against all evil.

Fortress:
stronghold
defense
mainstay

Prayer of Praise

Father, You are my strength and protection each day from the forces of evil and the power of the devil. Your wall of love surrounds me and provides a spiritual defense from the danger that lurks unnoticed all around me. I praise You, for in Your fortress I can rest assured of Your unfailing protection and constant love. Amen.

Personal Meditation

...You are awesome beyond words!

How awesome is the LORD Most High,
the great King over all the earth!
Psalm 47:2 (NIV)

Today's Truth:
God is the Lord Most High, yet He
knows me!

Awesome:
great
astonishing

Prayer of Praise

It is amazing to me that although You are the great King of all
the earth, yet You know me. You know my thoughts and feelings,
You see my attitude and actions, and still You love me. Wonder...
admiration...awe... my words are inadequate, for You and Your love are
indescribable. I pray that Your Holy Spirit will convey to You what
my words cannot adequately express, and give me words to share the
feelings I have for You with others that they too may come to know
You! Today and every day may I give You the highest place in my
heart, my mind, my thoughts and my life. Amen.

Personal Meditation

...You are worthy of my songs of adoration.

Sing out your praises to our God, our King.
Yes, sing your highest praises to our King,
the King of all the earth. Sing thoughtful praises!
Psalm 47:6-7 (LB)

Today's Truth:
God hears my songs of praise.

Sing:
chant
whistle
hum

Prayer of Praise

The wind whispers through the trees, the waves roll their gentle rhythm against the shore, the birds warble Your praise from early in the morning with the crow of the rooster, to late in the evening with the owl's hoot. Even as creation sings Your praise, I, too, Father, lift my voice to You with songs of highest praise and worship. Singing Your songs lifts me from the cares of this world as I focus not on what is around me, but on You and Your grace and infinite love for me! I close my eyes and "see" You as my audience of one, listening so lovingly to each word I sing. Amen.

Personal Meditation

...You are my faithful Guide for my entire life's journey.

For this great God is our God forever and ever.
He will be our guide until we die. Psalm 48:14
(LB)

Today's Truth:

God leads and guides me every day. He is
with me now and guides me always.

Guide:
leader
pilot
advisor

Prayer of Praise

Father, each day I face many challenges. It is comforting to know
that You direct and guide my decisions today, and You will continue
to advise me for all of my life. As my loving Father, You lead me
and show me the way. You are all-knowing with my best interests at
heart. Open my ears to hear Your voice directing me. Inspire me to be
more like You in all that I say and do. I praise You, such a great and
powerful God, that You chose to be my God forever and ever! Amen.

Personal Meditation

...You have redeemed my soul and offer me eternal life.

But God will redeem my life from the grave;
he will surely take me to himself. Selah.
Psalm 49:15 (NIV)

Today's Truth:

God alone has the power to redeem me from sin.
His Son Jesus atoned for all my sins, and through
His sacrifice offers me the gift of eternal life.

Redeem:
rescue
ransom
recover

Prayer of Praise

"O death, where is your victory? O death, where is your sting?"
1 Corinthians 15:55 (NASB) Father, these scripture verses remind me
that You have rescued me from sin and its penalties, one of which is
death. Praise be to You, Jesus, for redeeming me by paying the price
for my sins, so that one day I may cross over into heaven with joy,
peace and excitement! Amen.

Personal Meditation

...You are my Sustainer.

*Surely God is my help; the Lord
is the one who sustains me.
Psalm 54:4 (NIV)*

Today's Truth:
My faith and my relationship with God
are nourished as I read His Holy Word.

Sustain:
nourish
support
uphold

Prayer of Praise

You have established a way for me. When I feel like my spiritual feet
are slipping off Your path for me, I praise You; You are always there
to keep me from sinking and falling. You uphold me spiritually.
Through Your Holy Word You provide wisdom and understanding
which nourishes my faith and enriches my relationship with You. You
show me so much love and compassion. I praise You for Your kindness
toward me. Amen.

Personal Meditation

...You hear my cry and rush to save me.

But I call to God, and the LORD saves me.
Evening, morning and noon I cry out
in distress, and he hears my voice.
Psalm 55:16-17 (NIV)

Today's Truth:
The Lord God knows my thoughts and
hears my cries. He will save me!

Save:
spare
keep
preserve

Prayer of Praise

The enemy of my soul is Satan. He tries desperately, Father, to make
me love You less and grow cold in my desire to know You better. You
have reversed his plans. When I cry out to You, You fill me with a
desire to read Your Word more, and You give me an inner joy and
peace. You have defeated him, Jesus, by dying on the cross and rising
from the dead, and You are in heaven right now interceding for me.
Praise be to You that I am saved! Amen.

Personal Meditation

Day 135

...You carry my burdens.

Give your burdens to the Lord. He will carry them.
He will not permit the godly to slip or fall.
Psalm 55:22 (LB)

Today's Truth:
I will not fall under the weight of my burdens
because the Lord carries them for me!

Burden:
pressure
load
weight

Prayer of Praise

Father, sometimes I pressure myself, I try to accomplish too much, and then I become overwhelmed with life. At other times, others place expectations upon me and I feel I have no control over anything. Then I remember that there is no difficulty that Your Son Jesus did not face when He lived on earth. How marvelous to know that I am not alone and that there is no burden You cannot carry. Please help me to give my burdens to You in prayer and then not take them back again, but to trust in You, knowing that there is no difficulty in my life that You cannot carry me through, change or release me from. Amen.

Personal Meditation

...You always walk with me and offer constant protection and strength.

O my Strength, I watch for you; you, O God,
are my fortress, my loving God.
Psalm 59:9-10a (NIV)

Today's Truth:
As I watch for God to come, I can trust in
His enduring love.

Watch:
vigil
lookout

Prayer of Praise

In my mind's eye, Father, I am standing on the wall of Your fortress surrounding me, watching for You to come. From the height of the wall I look intently for You as I call, "Lord Jesus, come and save me right now–this very moment–from the heartache I am feeling!" And so You come, miraculously, quietly, quickly; in my spirit, I know You are there! I praise You for the rush of love I sense. My tears of praise flow because You always walk with me. Your presence in my life is real. I do indeed watch for You today! Amen.

Personal Meditation

...You are my place of safety each day.

But as for me, I will sing each morning about your power
and mercy. For you have been my high tower of refuge,
a place of safety in the day of my distress.
Psalm 59:16 (LB)

Today's Truth:
With assurance I begin each morning
knowing God will provide a place of safety
for me.

Safety:
assurance
security
surety

Prayer of Praise

I can begin each day under Your gracious care because, my loving God, You always go before me! Some days I feel more vulnerable to the attacks of my enemy, Satan. I praise You for being my refuge. Your Word gives me a spiritual armor against my struggles with sin and lifts me to a place of safety. In You I can regain my strength and confidence. Thank You for the blessings of each new morning! Amen.

Personal Meditation

...You bless my soul with rest and offer salvation.

My soul finds rest in God alone; my salvation comes from him.
Psalm 62:1 (NIV)

Today's Truth:

God has gained the victory for me. I can rest in His love and enjoy the peace I feel.

Rest:
repose
relief
comfort

Prayer of Praise

Lord, some days life seems overwhelming! Thank You for the comfort and quiet I find in You. My relief comes from knowing that salvation is mine. I praise You because heaven awaits me, because You, Jesus, became the perfect sacrifice for my sins. Hallelujah! Amen.

Personal Meditation

...You alone give victory over struggles in my life.

But I stand silently before the Lord, waiting for him to rescue me. For salvation comes from him alone. Yes, he alone is my Rock, my rescuer, defense and fortress—why then should I be tense with fear when troubles come?
Psalm 62:5-6 (LB)

Today's Truth:
God alone is my Savior.

Alone:
only
sole

Prayer of Praise

Heavenly Father, You are like a huge rock that is solid and secure. On You I stand, because You are immovable, nothing can break You apart. You are my Rescuer, I trust in You to save me from all danger. No circumstance can move You from my side. You are my Defense when Satan comes to accuse me; You protect me and thwart his attacks. You guard me from the world's harm. You are my Fortress; I have such confidence when surrounded by Your wall of love. You alone are all I need in this life. Amen.

Personal Meditation

...You influence my life and offer salvation.

My salvation and my honor depend on God; he is my mighty rock, my refuge.
Psalm 62:7 (NIV)

Today's Truth:
God is the greatest influence in my life;
He offers salvation.

Depend:
rely
hinge

Prayer of Praise

As I stand quietly in Your presence, Lord Jesus, I marvel at Your love for me. Your love does not depend on my performance or my good deeds, but You love me unconditionally. I praise You for providing salvation for me. I am who I am because of You! I would not be the person I am if it weren't for Your influence in my life. The integrity of my life comes from You. Because You love me, I can love others. Amen.

Personal Meditation

Day 141

...You answer prayer.

And because you answer prayer, all mankind
will come to you with their requests.
Psalm 65:2 (LB)

Today's Truth:
God will answer me when I pray.

Request:
appeal
entreaty
petition

Prayer of Praise

Heavenly Father, You do great and amazing things every day... You cause the sun to rise each morning, send rain to water the earth, paint the sunsets each evening and hang the stars in the night sky. I marvel that a God so great hears me when I pray! You answer with "Yes," "No," or "Wait," but you always answer. Amen.

Personal Meditation

...When I ask, You forgive all my sins.

When we were overwhelmed by sins, you forgave our transgressions.
Psalm 65:3 (NIV)

Today's Truth:
God frees me from the weight of my sin.

Overwhelm:
crush
defeat

Prayer of Praise

Lord, all I need to do is ask forgiveness for any sin and the Bible says, "You forgive them all" (Psalm 65:3 LB). Even when sin overwhelms me, crushing me down, when sin has made a barrier between us, when I am bruised beneath its load… Your forgiveness frees me completely from the weight of my trespasses and washes me as white as snow. Thank You for Your grace that reconciles me to You. Amen.

Personal Meditation

...You made every mountain.

He formed the mountains by his mighty strength.
Psalm 65:6 (LB)

Today's Truth:
Mountains are huge, but God and His
love for me are even bigger!

Form:
build
create
shape

Prayer of Praise

God of all creation, by Your great power You created the mountains;
Your creation shows Your strength and power! No two mountain
ranges are the same, but all have amazing grandeur. Some can be
climbed while others, Father, stand as a reminder to me that only You
can conquer the seemingly unconquerable. Amen.

Personal Meditation

...You prepare the earth for us.

You care for the land and water it; you enrich it abundantly. The streams of God are filled with water to provide the people with grain, for so you have ordained it. You drench its furrows and level its ridges; you soften it with showers and bless its crops. You crown the year with your bounty, and your carts overflow with abundance. The grasslands of the desert overflow; the hills are clothed with gladness.
Psalm 65:9-12 (NIV)

Today's Truth:
God provides the earth and blesses it
with abundance for me!

Abundant:
ample
teeming
plentiful

Prayer of Praise

I glorify You, God the Creator, for providing all the beauty and bounty of nature. You give me so much more than I need or deserve. Your blessings are rich and free. You care for the earth and You care for me. I praise You for the abundance of all the earth. Father, Son, and Holy Spirit, how creative and wonderful You are! Amen.

Personal Meditation

Day 145

...You hold my life in Your hands.

*Praise our God, O peoples, let the sound of his praise be heard; he
has preserved our lives and kept our feet from slipping.*
Psalm 66:8-9 (NIV)

Today's Truth:
God preserves me in my daily life.

Preserve:
protect
keep
save

Prayer of Praise

Father, thank You for holding onto me, for being by my side holding
my hand, for lifting me up and carrying me when I can no longer go
on. With Your hands holding me securely, I cannot fail. Thank You for
establishing the path set before me and keeping me from tumbling
astray. It is comforting to know that You have ordained my life
especially for me. Hallelujah, my life is in Your care. Amen.

Personal Meditation

Day 146

....You have an eternal plan for all people to know You.

Send us around the world with the news of your
saving power and your eternal plan for all mankind.
Psalm 67:2 (LB)

Today's Truth:
I am a part of God's eternal plan when I
share the Good News with others!

Eternal:
timeless
ageless
enduring

Prayer of Praise

You are eternal... Father, Son, and Holy Spirit. I am blessed to be one among many people around the world that believe in You. I praise You that I heard and believed the Good News. Holy Spirit, give me the words to share the Good News with others that they too may know You as their Savior and dearest Friend. The plan You have for me continues without interruption; it is timeless. In the time You give me, may I bring praise and glory to You as I share Your Good News with others. Amen.

Personal Meditation

...You are a loving presence in my life.

Sing praises to the Lord! Raise your voice in song to him who rides upon the clouds! Jehovah is his name—oh, rejoice in his presence. He is a father to the fatherless; he gives justice to the widows, for he is holy.
Psalm 68:4-5 (LB)

Today's Truth:
I can trust in God's presence in all circumstances of my life.

Presence:
attendance
company

Prayer of Praise

Thank You, God, for providing for the fatherless and the widows, for all people who have experienced a loss. I pray that they feel Your presence in their lives. I know that trusting in You changes my entire perspective. I am no longer held captive by the grief or loneliness of this world but focus on You and Your love for me. I look forward to the day when I see You face to face and can then in person praise You and fall at Your feet in gratitude and worship. Amen.

Personal Meditation

...The lonely and imprisoned experience Your kindness and provision.

God sets the lonely in families and leads forth the prisoners with singing; but the rebellious live in a sun-scorched land.
Psalm 68:6 (NIV)

Today's Truth:
God is always there for me; when I am lonely, He comforts me.

Lonely:
desolate
solitary

Prayer of Praise

Some days, Father, I feel alone. Even when surrounded by people, I fear they do not fully understand. Help me to turn to You in my times of loneliness, because You know me better than anyone else. Please pull me out of my melancholy and help me to reach out to others in need in Your name. Because when I focus on You and others, I cannot help but feel the wonder of my blessings. Heavenly Father, thank You for my family, Christian friends, salvation, and freedom of religion. May You be lifted up and great praise be brought to You! Amen.

Personal Meditation

...You give me great joy.

The humble shall see their God at work for them. No wonder
they will be so glad! All who seek for God shall live in joy.
Psalm 69:32 (LB)

Today's Truth:
God is the genuine source of joy.

Joy:
delight
rapture
elation

Prayer of Praise

Triune God–Father, Son and Holy Spirit–You are my only and genuine source of lasting happiness. My joy comes from living my life in one accord with Your will. To know that the joy and happiness I experience here on earth is nothing to what I will experience in heaven is amazing! Amen

Personal Meditation

...You are my constant help and my only hope.

O Lord, you alone are my hope; I've trusted you from childhood. Yes, you have been with me from birth and have helped me constantly—no wonder I am always praising you!
Psalm 71:5-6 (LB)

Today's Truth:
God's love is constant and unconditional.

Constant:
steady
loyal
faithful

Prayer of Praise

Faithful Friend and Savior, You love me always, unconditionally, no matter what. I have enjoyed a lifetime of blessings. As I look back, I see Your constant presence in my life. I have learned that I can trust You. I look to the future with such great confidence, knowing that wherever, whenever I turn to You, You will be there for me, leading me home. Amen.

Personal Meditation

...You give me strength for each day.

I walk in the strength of the Lord God. I tell everyone
that you alone are just and good.
Psalm 71:16 (LB)

Today's Truth:
Each day God provides me with
the strength to serve Him.

Strength:
power
influence
energy

Prayer of Praise

Father in heaven, You are my strength each day. With energy and a
feeling of hope and promise I awake each morning to serve You!
Thank You that my faith in You influences how I view the challenges I
face. With confidence I move onward, knowing that You are beside me
keeping me free from harm. Please guard my heart and increase my
faith today and every day. By Your grace may my life be a testimony to
You and bring others to come to know You as I do. Amen.

Personal Meditation

...You guide and counsel me.

*You will keep on guiding me all my life with your wisdom and
counsel; and afterwards receive me into the glories of heaven!*
Psalm 73:24 (LB)

Today's Truth:
God's Word provides me with His counsel.

Counsel:
advise
guide
instruct

Prayer of Praise

Father, by Your great wisdom You counsel me. I can look back on my
life and see Your presence leading me onward. Your Word is full of
instruction and promises. Please open my ears to hear and heed Your
wise words of advice. I am confident of Your guidance in my life. One
day, when it is in Your perfect time, You will bring me home into the
glories of heaven. I look forward with joy to serve You forever in Your
kingdom! Amen.

Personal Meditation

...You remain my God forever.

*My health fails; my spirits droop, yet God remains! He is the
strength of my heart; he is mine forever.*
Psalm 73:26 (LB)

Today's Truth:
God's faithfulness and strength
will never fail me.

Remain:
stay
abide
endure

Prayer of Praise

Dearest Heavenly Father, thank You for remaining with me always
as my Confidante and Friend. When I am burdened by sickness or
the stress of the world, You rescue me. When my own courage and
strength fail, Yours is sufficient for me. When fear overwhelms me, You
keep me close, and I feel Your presence surrounding me. You give me
dear Christian friends to walk along with me; You give me Your love
unconditionally. Oh, yes, I will indeed tell others of Your exceedingly
wonderful deeds in my life! Amen.

Personal Meditation

...You are the God of day and night, summer and winter.

The day is yours, and also the night; you established the sun and moon. It was you who set all the boundaries of the earth; you made both summer and winter.
Psalm 74:16-17 (NIV)

Today's Truth:
God is there for me in all seasons and all times of the day.

Set:
arrange
regulate
establish

Prayer of Praise

God the Creator, it is comforting to know that You will bless each twenty-four hours with the warmth and brightness of day and cool darkness of night. There is security in knowing that You regulate the seasons. Spring brings the freshness of the first green leaves, and the heat and intensity of the summer sun encourages crops to grow. In autumn, the bold orange and vibrant red leaves brighten the trees, and the crisp, cold snow of winter paints landscapes of white. I praise You that throughout each day and in every season Your presence is made known by Your awesome creation. Amen.

Personal Meditation

...You display righteous anger.

You alone are to be feared. Who can stand before
you when you are angry?
Psalm 76:7 (NIV)

Today's Truth:
God expresses righteous anger, yet is
gracious and merciful to me.

Anger:
enrage
fury
ire

Prayer of Praise

Father, I praise You for being a God who is not indifferent to the
injustice and evil You see every day. I praise You for displaying an
anger that is perfect and totally just and yet remaining merciful and
gracious. Oh may I hate wrong and injustice as deeply as You do, dear
Savior. Amen.

Personal Meditation

...You are a God of miracles.

Your ways, O God, are holy. What god is so great as
our God? You are the God who performs miracles;
you display your power among the peoples.
Psalm 77:13-14 (NIV)

Today's Truth:
God's miracles boost my faith and
give me hope.

Miracle:
marvel
wonder

Prayer of Praise

Father, I praise You for all Your miracles. Miracles give hope; in
them I can see Your faithfulness, because nothing is outside of Your
knowledge and ability. What a comfort to realize You are always
watching, always alert to the happenings of my world. When life seems
overwhelming and my faith is wavering, I think of the miracles You
have performed, and my faith is buoyed and my focus is re-centered on
You! Most of all I praise You for the greatest miracle of all... salvation.
Amen.

Personal Meditation

...You guide me safely through each day.

But he led forth his own people like a flock,
guiding them safely through the wilderness.
Psalm 78:52 (LB)

Today's Truth:

God will bring me safely through
the challenges of each day.

Safely:

secure

unharmed

Prayer of Praise

Father, You are the same today as You were ages ago. Just as You led Your beloved Israel through difficult places and circumstances, so You lead me today. Each day brings new challenges and difficulties; please help me to follow You not only with my words, but my heart, trusting in You always. I praise You because nothing is too difficult for You. I am so glad You are my Shepherd and carefully guard and guide me today and every day. Amen.

Personal Meditation

...You alone will judge the earth.

*Stand up, O God, and judge the earth. For all of it
belongs to you. All nations are in your hands.*
Psalm 82:8 (LB)

Today's Truth:
By God's grace I am saved!

Judge:
evaluate
decide
appraise

Prayer of Praise

I praise You because You are the Perfect Judge. Father, You know all
my sins, yet You love me so much that You sent Your one and only Son,
Jesus Christ, to die for me. I praise You, Jesus, for taking the sentence
pronounced against me and nailing it to the cross! One day You will
return to judge the earth according to perfect evidence. It is with joy
that I know by God's grace alone I have been declared acquitted of my
sins by Your perfect sacrificial death on the cross. Hallelujah to the
Lamb! Amen.

Personal Meditation

...You protect me and give me wonderful blessings.

For the LORD God is a sun and shield; the LORD bestows favor and honor; no good thing does he withhold from those whose walk is blameless.
Psalm 84:11 (NIV)

Today's Truth:
God blesses me with every good thing!

Bestow:
award
present
donate

Prayer of Praise

God Almighty, You shed light on my path, penetrating the darkness and revealing the ways of the world that are contrary to Your will. You are my shield, protecting me from harm and danger. Thank You for blessing me with your approval and bestowing good upon me that I do not deserve. Your continual support and love help me to grow in strength of character and in faith. May the life I lead bring glory and honor to You. Amen.

Personal Meditation

...You rule with fairness, righteousness and love.

Your throne is founded on two strong pillars—the one is Justice and the other Righteousness. Mercy and Truth walk before you as your attendants.
Psalm 89:14 (LB)

Today's Truth:
God gives mercy and grace to me.

Founded:
supported
rooted
established

Prayer of Praise

Gracious Father, You are perfect. Your kingdom is rooted in fairness, truth and love. I praise You that in Your eyes, because of Jesus' death and resurrection, You see me as a new creation, because there is no way I could measure up. Thank You for the unmerited and undeserved grace and mercy You freely give me. Please help me to treat others as You do, keeping my words and actions rooted in fairness and love, seeking the truth and offering forgiveness. Amen.

Personal Meditation

...You are without beginning or end.

Lord, through all generations you have been our home!
Before the mountains were created, before the earth was formed,
you are God without beginning or end.
Psalm 90:1-2 (LB)

Today's Truth:
God is infinite and ageless.

Ageless:
timeless
perpetual
infinite

Prayer of Praise

Alpha and Omega, You are completely unrestricted by time or place. Where I am bound by time, You are timeless. I was conceived at a fixed point in history, but You have always been. You will continue without interruption, whereas I will die a physical death and live forever with You in paradise. You are infinite and ageless, yet You know me and You love me... oh the wonder of it all! Amen.

Personal Meditation

...You are not bound by time.

You speak, and man turns back to dust. A thousand years are but as
yesterday to you! They are like a single hour!
Psalm 90:3-4 (LB)

Today's Truth:
God grants me each new day.

Time:
period
moment
interval

Prayer of Praise

Father, time seems to be flying by for me, each year goes faster than
the one before. I cannot imagine that a thousand years are as a day,
a blink, a breath to You. I am given each moment only by Your grace.
Please help me to make the most of the time You give me, sharing Your
Word and love with others. When I return to dust—well, then I will be
home with You! Amen.

Personal Meditation

...You will always be my safe place.

I will say of the LORD, "He is my refuge and my
fortress, my God, in whom I trust."
Psalm 91:2 (NIV)

Today's Truth:
I can trust in God to be my
refuge.

Refuge:
safe place
haven
retreat

Prayer of Praise

There are so many changes in my world, Father, but You are always
present, constant and trustworthy. You are a safe refuge where I can
experience peace and comfort. Father, I have truly found You to be my
safe place, my protection, my sanctuary. You have brought relief and
lessened my difficulties. I trust in You alone. Amen.

Personal Meditation

Day 164

...Your promises serve as impenetrable armor.

For he rescues you from every trap, and protects you from the fatal plague. He will shield you with his wings! They will shelter you. His faithful promises are your armor.
Psalm 91:3-4 (LB)

Today's Truth:
God's promises are an armor
that defend and protect me.

Armor:
defense
protection
covering

Prayer of Praise

Father, I praise You for each promise You have given me in Your Word. Your promises serve as my armor, carrying me through all the dangers and fears of life, equipping me with a sure defense against worry and all evil. I am covered with Your love, knowing that You are my Savior, that You will never leave or forsake me, and that all my sins have been forgiven. Thank You for Your promises written in Your Holy Bible. I entrust myself to Your protection and pledge my devotion to You! Amen.

Personal Meditation

...You instruct your angels to guard and steady me.

For he orders his angels to protect you wherever you go. They will steady you with their hands to keep you from stumbling against the rocks on the trail.
Psalm 91:11-12 (LB)

Today's Truth:
God loves me so much that He sends
His angels to guard and protect me.

Order:
command
instruct

Prayer of Praise

Father, I praise You for commanding Your faithful angels to watch over me. Thank You for sending them to be beside me guarding and steadying me. Thank You for instructing Your angels to protect me from the world's influences, Satan's pitfalls, and myself. It is comforting to know that You, God, watch over me, taking care of my needs and are always protecting me. Amen.

Personal Meditation

...You know my thoughts.

The LORD knows the thoughts of man; he knows that they are futile.
Psalm 94:11 (NIV)

Today's Truth:
With God's help I can focus on the things that are important!

Futile:
vain
hopeless
empty

Prayer of Praise

Father, often my thoughts are useless, accomplishing no real purpose. I worry about things that do not really matter. I fixate on minute details or I waste my energy in thoughts that are trite and shallow, vain and hopeless. But given to You and empowered by Your Holy Spirit, I can ask for the very mind of Christ. I pray that You would make my thoughts like Your thoughts, and I know that it will follow that my words and actions will be pleasing to You! Please help me to focus and think on You and Your love for me. Amen.

Personal Meditation

You control everything.

For the Lord is a great God, the great King of all gods.
He controls the formation of the depths of the earth
and the mightiest mountains; all are his.
Psalm 95:3-4 (LB)

Today's Truth:
God who manages everything
loves me.

Control:
rule
manage
direct

Prayer of Praise

Father, in other countries people worship gods of stone and wood. I praise You that You are alive, and by Your Holy Spirit, living within my heart! It amazes me to realize how loved I am by the One who developed, and continues to control and sustain all that my eyes can take in. Amen.

Personal Meditation

You are my Shepherd.

*Come, let us bow down in worship, let us kneel before
the LORD our Maker; for he is our God and we are the people
of his pasture, the flock under his care.*
Psalm 95:6-7 (NIV)

Today's Truth:
God cares for me as a
shepherd cares for his sheep.

Shepherd:
leader
pastor

Prayer of Praise

Father, You are my Shepherd. Just as a shepherd cares for his sheep,
You gently care for me, You lovingly guide me. I hear Your voice in my
soul calling me safely to Your side. You protect me from the dangers
of the world. You nurture and encourage me. You take care of all of my
needs. When I go astray, You seek me out and lead me back to safety.
Thank You for shepherding me so that I may grow in my faith and
follow You! Amen.

Personal Meditation

You do marvelous and amazing things.

Publish his glorious acts throughout the earth. Tell everyone about the amazing things he does. For the Lord is great beyond description, and greatly to be praised.
Psalm 96:3-4 (LB)

Today's Truth:
God is so great that my praise
for Him overflows.

Amazing:
overwhelming
astonishing
impressive

P r a y e r   o f   P r a i s e

You are beyond description, Father! You are wonderful…
remarkable…supernatural…miraculous…splendid…extraordinary…
astonishing…surprising … I am overwhelmed by all that You have
done and the blessings You continue to give to me. My heart is full
of appreciation for Your goodness. I give You all my praise. I will
continue to tell others about You and Your greatness. Amen.

Personal Meditation

Dignity and beauty surround You.

Honor and majesty surround him; strength and beauty are in his Temple.
Psalm 96:6 (LB)

Today's Truth:
In heaven I will experience the fullness of God's glory.

Honor:
dignity
reverence
respect

Prayer of Praise

Loving Father, I cannot begin to imagine the reverence and beauty that surrounds You in Your heavenly Home. On earth, I occasionally glimpse something so beautiful that I think that maybe I've seen a little bit of what heaven must be like. I look forward to the day that You welcome me into Your awesome presence, surrounded by Your glory and dominion. On that day, I will sing praises with all the saints and dance with joy just to see You face to face. Until then, Father, I will share the Good News of Your love with others. Amen.

Personal Meditation

Everything created
displays Your greatness!

Let the heavens be glad, the earth rejoice; let the vastness of the roaring seas demonstrate his glory. Praise him for the growing fields, for they display his greatness. Let the trees of the forest rustle with praise.
Psalm 96:11-12 (LB)

Today's Truth:
God's creation reveals His greatness.

Display:
reveal
uncover
expose

Prayer of Praise

God of all, sometimes Your greatness breaks forth suddenly like a mighty lightning bolt in the dark night sky, and other times in quiet splendor when the sunset sky changes colors again and again. Rolling fields of grain and the great variety of trees also display your greatness. How is it that people cannot believe in You when they see the evidence of Your greatness? Please give me the words coupled with Your displays of wonder to lead others to know You and love You as I do. Amen.

Personal Meditation

Day 172

You keep protective watch over the faithful.

Let those who love the LORD hate evil, for he guards the lives of his faithful ones and delivers them from the hand of the wicked.
Psalm 97:10 (NIV)

Today's Truth:
God guards my life and protects me from sin and evil.

Guard:
watch
defend
protect

Prayer of Praise

Abba Father, I praise You for the tender care You provide to those who are Your children. All around me is unrighteousness. Sometimes it is blatant and easy to identify as sin, but at other times, Lord, evil can be so subtle and cunning, threatening to slip into my life unnoticed. I praise and thank You for guarding me against evil and for providing deliverance from sin, which can so easily ensnare. Give me Your hatred for any form of evil, no matter how socially acceptable, small or insignificant it may seem. Amen.

Personal Meditation

You will return and judge us perfectly.

Let the waves clap their hands in glee, and the hills sing out their songs of joy before the Lord, for he is coming to judge the world with perfect justice.
Psalm 98:8-9 (LB)

Today's Truth:
As a follower of God I will be victorious with Him when He judges the earth.

Glee:
delight
elation
merriment

Prayer of Praise

Perfect Judge, You have called us to appoint individuals to judge in our courts. Yet no judge in this world has the perfect wisdom and knowledge You possess to judge in absolute righteousness. I look forward to when You come on the Last Day and judge the world with absolute fairness and impartiality. With delight I praise You for the victory that You have already secured through the perfect life, death and resurrection of Jesus Christ. Amen.

Personal Meditation

Even the angels come and go at Your bidding.

The angels are his messengers—his servants of fire!
Psalm 104:4 (LB)

Today's Truth:
I can serve God by being a
messenger of His Good News.

Messenger:
herald
page
courier

Prayer of Praise

I praise You because everything is in Your control and serves You.
Even the angels quickly serve You when dispatched...like fire! When
You speak, may I also listen for Your voice directing me and quickly
do Your will. Holy Spirit, please give me the words that I may be a
messenger and share the Good News of Your love with others! Amen.

Personal Meditation

You created the earth full of variety.

O Lord, what a variety you have made! And in wisdom you have made them all! The earth is full of your riches.
Psalm 104:24 (LB)

Today's Truth:
God's wisdom and goodness are evident by the wide variety He created for my enjoyment and benefit.

Variety:
assortment
diversity

Prayer of Praise

I praise You for the wide and diverse variety in Your creation! In wisdom You have made all there ever has been, all there is, and all that is yet to be. In goodness You have provided everything that I need to sustain my life. Help me be a steward of the earth, caring for the gifts You have created. Please help me see the uniqueness that surrounds me in the people I meet and in myself. Help me to become more aware of the special talents and abilities that You have blessed me with, that I may use them to praise Your glorious name. Amen.

Personal Meditation

Your goodness is evident all around me.

He is the Lord our God. His goodness is seen everywhere throughout the land.
Psalm 105:7 (LB)

Today's Truth:
God's goodness surrounds me.

Goodness:
blessing
kindness
generosity

Prayer of Praise

Everywhere I look, Father, I see Your goodness. Your faithfulness in the rising of the sun... Your provision in the rain... Your lavish creativity in the beauty of the earth You have given as my home. For these and all the blessings that surround me, I give You praise. You certainly are "the Lord our God!" Amen.

Personal Meditation

Your name is powerful and above every name.

Blessed is his name forever and forever. Praise him from sunrise to sunset! For he is high above the nations; his glory is far greater than the heavens.
Psalm 113:2-4 (LB)

Today's Truth:
God's goodness surrounds me.

Blessed:
divine
sacred
hallowed

Prayer of Praise

Just speaking Your name... Jesus... Jesus...Jesus... brings quietness to my soul. What a day that will be for me, when I bow humbly before You and utter Your name... Jesus...Jesus...precious Jesus! Yes, the Lord Jesus Christ, the Lord Jesus Christ! Your name has power over Satan. Your name brings healing. And at Your name, one day every knee will bow and confess that You are Lord! Amen.

Personal Meditation

You lift up the needy, setting them in a better place.

Who can be compared with God enthroned on high? Far below him are the heavens and the earth; he stoops to look, and lifts the poor from the dirt, and the hungry from the garbage dump, and sets them among princes!
Psalm 113:5-8 (LB)

Today's Truth:
In God's eyes I have value.
His love raises me to heaven.

Lift:
elevate
boost
raise

Prayer of Praise

Father, I praise You for caring for the poor, hungry and needy! Lift them again today from the "garbage dump"; and lift me too, who, though I have food, allow many other forms of "garbage," to invade my life. Hallelujah for a Father who cleanses me from all "garbage," lifting me to a higher place. Amen.

Personal Meditation

Even from the highest heaven, You hear my prayers.

I love the Lord because he hears my prayers and answers them. Because he
bends down and listens, I will pray as long as I breathe!
Psalm 116:1-2 (LB)

Today's Truth:
God listens carefully and
answers each of my prayers.

Listen:
hear
concentrate

Prayer of Praise

In the quietness of my time with You, dear Father, I know I am loved...I
know I am accepted... I know You listen to me. I praise You for always
being there for me. I realize that there is nothing high enough or deep
enough or wide enough to keep You from hearing me when I pray.
Thank You for listening carefully and giving Your undivided attention
to each of my prayers. Amen.

Personal Meditation

When I need immediate help, You are there.

In my distress I prayed to the Lord and he answered me and rescued me.
He is for me! How can I be afraid? What can mere man do to me?
Psalm 118:5-6 (LB)

Today's Truth:
God takes care of all of my
worries.

Distress:
worry
agony
trouble

Prayer of Praise

Father, life brings situations that can cause worry and anxiety. How I praise You that right now, this very moment, I can give You my anxious thoughts and immediately You put my mind at rest. No matter where I am when I call out to You, You meet me there. You are so good to me! Amen.

Personal Meditation

I know You always support me.

The LORD is my strength and my song; he has become my salvation.
Psalm 118:14 (NIV)

Today's Truth:
God nurtures and develops my faith.

Become:
grow
change
develop

Prayer of Praise

Father, when my faith was young, You were my strength and my song.
By Your grace, my faith has grown and my relationship with You has
been nurtured and developed. You are still my strength and my song,
but You have become my salvation—not only my spiritual salvation, but
also my daily deliverance from sin, and the power of the devil. How I
praise You that my faith is founded in You. Amen.

Personal Meditation

Day 182

...You protect me in the midst of a crisis.

You are my refuge and my shield, and your
promises are my only source of hope.
Psalm 119:114 (LB)

Today's Truth:
It is in God's loving promises that
our hope exists.

Promise:
pledge
assurance

Prayer of Praise

Father, when I need shelter from the storm, You are there. In Your
promises I will rest! You are all I need. You are my protector...my
strength...my shield and my hope. Amen.

Personal Meditation

...The Truth of Your Word enables my understanding.

Your laws are wonderful; no wonder I obey them. As your plan
unfolds, even the simple can understand it.
Psalm 119:129-130 (LB)

Today's Truth:
God's Word gives insight and
discernment.

Unfolds:
develops
is clarified
is disclosed

Prayer of Praise

Father, I marvel at Your Word! Your Holy Spirit is my Teacher, who
gives me glimpses of Your heavenly plan. As You guide me into Truth,
I gain a deeper understanding of Your ways, and in so doing I see they
are so right and so good! Amen.

Personal Meditation

...What You require of me is to the point and fitting for me.

Your demands are just and right.
Psalm 119:138 (LB)

Your justice is eternal for your laws are perfectly fair.
Psalm 119:142 (LB)

Today's Truth:
God's justice can only be measured from the perspective of His throne.

Demands:
requirements
statutes

Prayer of Praise

Father, I am growing in my understanding that Your plan for me is correct and suitable. Your Word continues on and on...it lasts forever. As I grow in You, I find its truths are logical. What You dispense in justice is independent of time. What You ask of me stems from the sea of logic that only a just God fully understands. Amen.

Personal Meditation

...Your will is consistent.

I have known from earliest days that your will never changes.
Psalm 119:152 (LB)

Today's Truth:
God does not adjust to us; we
must adjust to God.

Will:
specific purpose
determination

Prayer of Praise

How wonderful it has been, Father, to know that Your plan and
purposes stand firm; they do not change with time or the whims of
people. You are to be praised again today for Your mercy on me. Your
will is perfect and Your goodness will last for all eternity. Amen.

Personal Meditation

...You will keep Your promises to the generations that follow me.

Your faithfulness continues through all generations;
you established the earth, and it endures.
Psalm 119:90 (NIV)

Today's Truth:
God's faithfulness lives on,
prevailing into eternity.

Extends:
continues
reaches

Prayer of Praise

You, oh God, are faithful! Your covenant is everlasting! It is in the assurance of Your promises that I stand. May I proclaim this truth to all those around me, that they too may rejoice in You, the God who sustains His people and whose faithfulness is timeless.

Personal Meditation

...You preserve me in every circumstance.

The Lord will keep you from all harm–he will watch over your life;
the Lord will watch over your coming and going both now and forevermore.
Psalm 121:3-8 (NIV)

Today's Truth:
God is an intimate God who loves and
protects His children.

Preserve:
protect
shelter
care for

Prayer of Praise

Oh, Father, You are ever watchful. Therefore, it is with confidence that I act, and with assurance that I rest, knowing Your hand of protection is upon me. All my trust is in You, just as a child who reaches for her father's hand in the dark. I know You are there to guide and sustain me. Hallelujah! Amen.

Personal Meditation

...No matter where I am, You provide watchful care over me.

Our help is from the Lord who made heaven and earth.
Psalm 124:8 (LB)

Today's Truth:

The magnificent Creator of the universe,
Jehovah God, cares for me.

Care:
concern
attention
diligence

Prayer of Praise

I know, Father, that You encircle me on all sides. I praise You for dwelling within me by Your Holy Spirit. Your protective watch assures me that I am NEVER beyond Your sight, reach or touch. It is a blessing to think that You, who created the heavens and the earth, are a border around me! Amen.

Personal Meditation

...You are good!

Oh give thanks to the LORD, for he is good;
his lovingkindness continues forever.
Psalm 136:1 (LB)

Today's Truth:
God is no respecter of persons; He loves
all of His creation equally.

lovingkindness:
compassionate love

Prayer of Praise

Father, since You are eternal and in charge of everything, I sure am
thankful that You are good! You have promised to love all You have
created–every nation of every color in every tongue. Though in this
world we may experience suffering and discrimination, we also know
and experience Your compassion and goodness! Amen.

Personal Meditation

...You provide even my food.

He gives food to every living thing, for his
lovingkindness continues forever.
Psalm 136:25 (LB)

Today's Truth:
God meets my necessities,
including daily bread.

Sustenance:
nourishment
food

Prayer of Praise

Dear God, more and more I find I am happiest in my dependency upon
You. You, God, are the source of all that nourishes me. I praise You
for giving me things to eat, but also for feeding my soul. Your Word
gives my spirit strength, and by Your grace You provide for my physical
body. Amen.

Personal Meditation

...Though You are great, You have concern for the poor.

Yes, they shall sing about Jehovah's glorious ways, for his glory is very great. Yet though he is so great, he respects the humble, but proud men must keep their distance.
Psalm 138:5-6 (LB)

But the Lord will surely help those they persecute; he will maintain the rights of the poor.
Psalm 140:12 (LB)

Today's Truth:
We serve a glorious God Who respects the humble and defends the poor.

Respect:
to show concern and high regard

Prayer of Praise

Father, although Your glory is vast, You are still the defender of the poor and the endless supplier of their needs. For Your joy, Oh Lord, is not found in our financial status but in the humility of those who choose to follow You. Lord, keep me humble, that my life may sing more of Your glorious ways. Amen.

Personal Meditation

Day 192

…You alone are my place of refuge.

I cry to you, O LORD; I say, "You are my refuge,
my portion in the land of the living."
Psalm 142:5 (NIV)

Today's Truth:
Sincere trust and dependence upon
God completes our rest.

Refuge:
shelter from distress

Prayer of Praise

Lord as I focus more on You, the noises of the world all around me are
made quiet. Father, with You I know peace, and in You I find my safe
refuge. To know You, Lord, is sufficient. You fulfill my needs. Bless
you Lord. Amen.

Personal Meditation

...You are an amazing God!

Great is Jehovah! Greatly praise him! His greatness is beyond discovery!
Psalm 145:3 (LB)

Your awe-inspiring deeds shall be on every tongue; I will proclaim your greatness.
Everyone will tell about how good you are, and sing about your righteousness.
Jehovah is kind and merciful, slow to get angry, full of love.
Psalm 145:6-8 (LB)

Today's Truth:
If our eyes are open... God's greatness
cannot be overlooked!

Awe-Inspiring:
causing overwhelming
admiration

Prayer of Praise

I cannot, as hard as I may try, uncover and define Your greatness. All of creation proclaims Your greatness! In this I am overwhelmed. I praise Your kindness, mercy and love, but it is in Your amazing greatness that I marvel! Remove from me anything in my life that fails to reflect Your glory. Amen.

Personal Meditation

...Your love is intertwined in Your deeds of kindness.

He is good to everyone, and his compassion is intertwined with everything he does.
Psalm 145:9 (LB)

For your kingdom never ends. You rule generation after generation.
Psalm 145:13 (LB)

Today's Truth:
God's deeds are built upon the framework
of His compassion.

Intertwined:
interlaced

Prayer of Praise

Your love for me surrounds and encompasses me. Compassion is interlaced in Your precious Word. As the trellis supports a climbing vine, so too does my life intertwine and depend upon You and Your compassionate ways. I wrap my thoughts around You. I reach out for You in the words that I may speak and lean upon You for the works that I do. As the winter of my life approaches, it is You, my trellis, I pray that others may see. Amen.

Personal Meditation

...When I fall, You are there to lift me up.

The Lord lifts the fallen and those bent beneath their
loads. The eyes of all mankind look up to you for help;
you give them their food as they need it.
Psalm 145:14-15 (LB)

Today's Truth:
Life's burdens are eased as we trust in God.

Bent:
burdened

Prayer of Praise

Loving God, I know that sometimes You choose not to remove the burdens we are carrying, but You always are there to provide the strength and nourishment we need to keep moving forward. When I do fall, You are there to lift my head...that I may see that it is in Your footsteps that I must follow. Follow You I will! Amen.

Personal Meditation

...You are always there when I come to You.

He is close to all who call on him sincerely. He fulfills the desires of those who reverence and trust him; he hears their cries for help and rescues them.
Psalm 145:18-19 (LB)

Today's Truth:
God's loving presence is always near for those who trust and obey Him.

Sincerely:
genuinely

Prayer of Praise

Father, today I long to see Your face, to look into Your eyes, to see Your nail-pierced hands. I love You and I worship You. I know Your ear is always close, and Your constant loving heart is quick to forgive. When I call out to You, You are there to grant to me the desires of Your will. Amen.

Personal Meditation

...You promise to provide for those in need.

He is the God who keeps every promise, and gives justice to the poor and oppressed, and food to the hungry. He frees the prisoners, and opens the eyes of the blind; he lifts the burdens from those bent down beneath their loads. For the Lord loves good men.
Psalm 146:6b-8 (LB)

Today's Truth:
God's overwhelming love cares for all.

Oppressed:
crushed

Prayer of Praise

Precious Savior, I was a prisoner to sin, but You have freed me. I was blind in many different ways, but because of Your grace I now see. I see the joy of Your heart in those who sing Your praises. I see the strength of Your love in those who forgive, and I see Your peace in those who trust in You. Lord, I desire to see more of You. Amen.

Personal Meditation

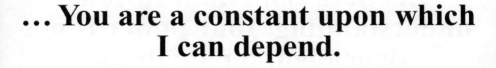

Day 198

... You are a constant upon which I can depend.

The LORD reigns forever, your God, O Zion, for all generations. Praise the LORD.
Psalm 146:10 (NIV)

Today's Truth:
God has no equal.

Reign:
exercise power

Prayer of Praise

You are a God Who has always reigned and always will, yet You love me. When I am in despair, Your love covers my grief and is the source of my healing. Your authority endures forever and in this constant I can be secure. Oh God, there is none like You. Amen.

Personal Meditation

...There is no limit to Your understanding. Your power is not dependent on anything.

He counts the stars and calls them all by name.
How great he is! His power is absolute!
His understanding is unlimited.
Psalm 147:4-5 (LB)

Today's Truth:
God is the source of all things. Power and knowledge flow from Him.

Absolute:
unquestionable

Prayer of Praise

Oh God, EVERY STAR HAS A NAME... EVERY STAR HAS A NUMBER... Is there no limit for You? Father, You are NOT dependent on anything—YET—everything is dependent on You! It is in Your unquestionable power and limitless knowledge that I trust– for surely You have no equal. Amen.

Personal Meditation

…You maintain and support all there is on earth.

He covers the sky with clouds; he supplies the earth with rain and makes grass grow on the hills. He provides food for the cattle and for the young ravens when they call.
Psalm 147:8-9 (NIV)

Today's Truth:
God lovingly cares for all He has created.

Maintain:
keep in proper condition

Prayer of Praise

You are the most glorious painter Whose brush is never still. As the artist Who cares for His handiwork, You care for all of Your creation. The composition of Your glorious works reflects Your heavenly throne. Help me, oh God, to be diligent in caring for Your precious creation. Amen.

Personal Meditation

...You send Your orders for everything!

He sends his orders to the world. How swiftly his word flies.
He sends the snow in all its lovely whiteness, and scatters the
frost upon the ground, and hurls the hail upon the earth. Who
can stand before his freezing cold?
Psalm 147:15-17 (LB)

Today's Truth:
All of nature is compelled by the
power of the living God.

Orders:
methodical arrangements

Prayer of Praise

Father, in Your creative wisdom You conduct all of creation to sing of
Your majesty. It is by Your orchestration that the elements move and by
Your hand that we exist. I pray, oh God, that I may never overlook the
glory of Your creation. Amen.

Personal Meditation

...Your official order made and established everything permanently.

Let everything he has made give praise to him. For he issued his command, and they came into being; he established them forever and forever. His orders will never be revoked.
Psalm 148:5-6 (LB)

Today's Truth:
In God's wisdom are all things created; nothing in creation will change outside of His will.

Established:
permanently fixed

Prayer of Praise

You, Father, are the ONLY predictable weatherman! You give the official orders and the weather does Your bidding. You fixed firmly the seasons, and in Your wisdom know how long each season will last. Forgive me for my grumbling, for I know that all of this is in Your hand alone. You have established them forever and ever. Amen.

Personal Meditation

...Nothing created is greater than You!

And praise him down here on earth, you creatures of the ocean depths. Let fire and hail, snow, rain, wind and weather, all obey. Let the mountains and hills, the fruit trees and cedars, the wild animals and cattle, the snakes and birds, the kings and all the people, with their rulers and their judges, young men and maidens, old men and children—all praise the Lord together. For he alone is worthy. His glory is far greater thanall of earth and heaven.
Psalm 148:7-13 (LB)

Today's Truth:

The Creator of all is worthy of the praise of all.

Alone:
without equal

Prayer of Praise

Oh Papa, Your creation is compelled to exalt You. There can be no equal. I await the glorious day when in unison all of mankind will bow before You in worship. For at Your feet every tongue from every tribe in every nation will proclaim Your glory. I can't wait for that moment! Amen.

Personal Meditation

...You enjoy me!

For Jehovah enjoys his people; he will save the humble. Let his people rejoice in this honor. Let them sing for joy as they lie upon their beds.
Psalm 149:4-5 (LB)

Today's Truth:
God of all creation takes joy
in His people

Enjoys:
takes pleasure in
to have full and satisfying use of

Prayer of Praise

Father it is profound to think that You take joy in me. This is a reaffirming fact of Your forgiving nature. By Your grace You have exchanged who I was for Who You are and I am humbled. You are the source of all my joy. You are my delight. Amen.

Personal Meditation

...You desire to pour out Your wisdom upon me.

Come here and listen to me! I'll pour out the spirit of wisdom upon you, and make you wise.
Proverbs 1:23 (LB)

Today's Truth:
God's wisdom is available to all who seek it.

Wisdom:
ability to discern what is true/right

Prayer of Praise

Father, You are Wisdom. Your wisdom is beyond my ability to take in and fully understand. In wisdom You create all... past, present and future. It is in the counsel of Your wisdom that I trust– for You also are my greatest Advisor! I find Your wisdom in the voice of a godly friend, in the heart of a loving pastor and in the pages of Your Word! Amen.

Personal Meditation

...You guard my mind and my way.

He grants good sense to the godly—his saints. He is their shield, protecting them and guarding their pathway. He shows how to distinguish right from wrong, how to find the right decision every time.
Proverbs 2:7-9 (LB)

Today's Truth:
God guards the steps of those in daily submission to Him.

Grants:
confers
bestows

Prayer of Praise

Father, You are sufficient and in You I am content, for:
>   You grant good sense.
>   Your hand of protection is upon me.
>   You guard the steps I take.
>   Your spirit reveals to me the difference between
>   right and wrong.
>   You fill my life with such joy as I walk in Your truth. Amen.

Personal Meditation

...Your counsel to me helps me to be spiritually healthy.

*Everything I say is right and true, for I hate lies
and every kind of deception. My advice is wholesome
and good. There is nothing of evil in it.
Proverbs 8:7-8 (LB)*

Today's Truth:
The character of God is our template.

Advice:
guidance for a
course of action

Prayer of Praise

Oh mighty God... As I set my life's course, I chart my path by You, my Compass. You are the only constant that I can rely on, and as my eyes are upon You, my path is clear, for Your ways are always right. You are my guiding path. Amen.

Personal Meditation

...Your instruction is worth more than anything.

Choose my instruction instead of silver, knowledge rather than choice gold, for wisdom is more precious than rubies, and nothing you desire can compare with her.
Proverbs 8:10-11 (NIV)

Today's Truth:
In God's bank is a storehouse of wisdom and instruction.

Instruction:
knowledge imparted

Prayer of Praise

Father, how I praise Your teachings, for Your wisdom has no equal. The material things which I value are worthless in comparison. Your wisdom can only be purchased with the currency of humility. God, place in me a desire to acquire more of You in my life. Amen.

Personal Meditation

...Your wisdom causes my day to be more productive and beneficial.

I, wisdom, dwell together with prudence;
I possess knowledge and discretion.
Proverbs 8:12 (NIV)

Today's Truth:
God's wisdom always reflects
care and discretion.

Prudence:
thoughtful care

Prayer of Praise

I praise You, Father, for being ALL-WISDOM. As I rely on Your knowledge and discretion, my day is more productive and my life more fulfilling. Dear God, this is my desire–to be useful in Your hands. Help me, Father, not to trust in my human wisdom but in true wisdom that flows from You and that reflects compassionate ways. Amen.

Personal Meditation

...You protect those who are Yours.

The way of the LORD is a refuge for the righteous,
but it is the ruin of those who do evil.
Proverbs 10:29 (NIV)

Today's Truth:
God is our safety and defender
of righteousness.

Protect:
guard

Prayer of Praise

Father, in Your hand I am safe. This is one thing I know. I praise Your
infinite mercy, for I am not deserving. But by Your goodness You have
granted to me the way of grace. I pray for those who refuse it... Bring
them to repentance that they too may know of Your goodness and
forsake their destructive path. Amen.

Personal Meditation

...You take pleasure in my kind words.

The Lord hates the thoughts of the wicked but delights in kind words.
Proverbs 15:26 (LB)

Today's Truth:
The kindness of the Father must flow from the lips of His children.

Kind:
tender

Prayer of Praise

My words cannot adequately praise You, Father. In You I stand amazed. It is profound to think the God of the universe delights in me and that I am one of Your children! I know my words are not always kind and fall short of Your character. May Your love flow from me more and more. May the words from Your heart flow from my lips. Amen.

Personal Meditation

...You bless me when I obey.

God blesses those who obey him;
happy the man who puts his trust in the Lord.
Proverbs 16:20 (LB)

Today's Truth:
Happiness is found in trust and obedience.

Obedience:
submission
compliance
respect

Prayer of Praise

I praise You because You want me to obey
    and serve You gladly in every way.
I choose You, dear Savior,
    to be my daily Guide...
For then there is nothing
    from which I must hide.

Father God, I count it a privilege to trust You...and to obey You!
Truly You make me happy. Amen.

Personal Meditation

...You are the truest Friend.

There are "friends" who pretend to be friends,
but there is a friend who sticks closer than a brother.
Proverbs 18:24 (LB)

Today's Truth:
Jesus Christ abides with His children
and sees them through all the
challenges they face.

sticks:
holds fast
endures

Prayer of Praise

Father, how easy it is to praise the One Who every day remains
loyal and faithful to me! In Your Word there are many examples
of deep friendships, both in families and among friends, where
individuals truly support one another. Your support, though, is so much
greater. You never leave me, but hold me fast and bring me through
disappointments and dangers, teaching me more about Yourself all
along the way. Amen.

Personal Meditation

...What You have spoken through Your Word is true.

*Every word of God is flawless; he is a shield
to those who take refuge in him.
Proverbs 30:5 (NIV)*

Today's Truth:
What God declares should come
to pass, comes to pass. His way is
sure, steadfast, and always the best.

flawless:
absolute
whole
errorless

Prayer of Praise

I have seen again and again that every promise You state in Your
Word proves genuine. Help me to trust more completely the truth of
all that You have spoken. Also, please bring me to readily rejoice in
the privilege I enjoy of being guided by You, the One Who knows all
things. I give glory to You today for being entirely reliable. Amen.

Personal Meditation

Day 215

...I can rely on You to defend me.

See, God has come to save me! I will trust
and not be afraid, for the Lord is my strength and song;
he is my salvation.
Isaiah 12:2 (LB)

Today's Truth:
Undoubtedly, God is my sanctuary.
He covers for me, upholds me, and
preserves me daily.

Defend:
act on behalf of
fight for
keep safe

Prayer of Praise

I give You my deepest praise for Your watch-care over me today. Only
You can offer true protection and aid. You shield me not only from
Satan and the threats of the world, but also from myself, which is often
my greatest challenge. It is marvelous that You welcome me to take
refuge in You. Amen.

Personal Meditation

...You will see me through to heaven.

Trust in the LORD forever, for the LORD,
the LORD, is the Rock eternal.
Isaiah 26:4 (NIV)

Today's Truth:
God is worthy of my undying
faith. He is termless, timeless,
and indestructible.

Eternal:
enduring forever
constant
unfading

Prayer of Praise

Father, how magnificent that You are the only One Who can put limits
on Yourself. I can walk confidently in Your ways because Your nature
is one of consistency. I love to serve One Who is outside of time
and Who is without end. No other being, person, place, or thing is
unceasing like You. Amen.

Personal Meditation

...You are the Master Teacher.

*The Lord of Hosts is a wonderful teacher
and gives the farmer wisdom.*
Isaiah 28:29 (LB)

Today's Truth:
God set up the world, knows
how it works, and gladly gives
wisdom to those who seek it.

Teacher:
one who trains by example
authority
counselor

Prayer of Praise

Many times, dear Father, I have witnessed farmers at work in their
fields—planting, cultivating, harvesting their crops. You alone give
to farmers the understanding and skill it takes to raise those crops, as
well as the water that brings in the harvest. I praise You that You give
wisdom, not only to farmers, but to all who ask it of You. Like a tiny
seed that matures and grows, You nourish, train, and trim back each of
us to be the best we can be. Amen.

Personal Meditation

...As You teach me to be obedient, I am blessed.

O Lord, your discipline is good
and leads to life and health.
Oh, heal me and make me live!
Isaiah 38:16 (LB)

Today's Truth:
Following God's ways brings
fullness to our lives.

Discipline:
rigorous training
correction

Prayer of Praise

Father God, I praise You for the many ways You not only continually challenge me to obey Your commands, but help me do so as well. You transform half-hearted efforts and spiritual underdevelopment into maturity and fullness of life. Thank You for working in my heart constantly to help me become the best that I can be! Amen.

Personal Meditation

...You will one day return to earth and rule.

Yes, the Lord God is coming with mighty power; he
will rule with awesome strength.
See, his reward is with him, to each as he has done.
Isaiah 40:10 (LB)

Today's Truth:
The Lord is coming back and
will reign forevermore.

Awesome:
of wonder mixed with fear
astonishing
dreadful

Prayer of Praise

What a day that will be, dear Father, when Jesus comes back to make
a final statement about His authority and position as the High King. It
is a magnificent and terrifying thought. With overwhelming wonder, I
exalt You—the One Who is mightily above all. I rejoice in being one
of Your children, called to do kingdom work for You. Amen.

Personal Meditation

...The wonders You perform are staggering!

When I came, why was there no one? When I called, why was there no one to answer? Was my arm too short to ransom you? Do I lack the strength to rescue you? By a mere rebuke I dry up the sea, I turn rivers into a desert; their fish rot for lack of water and die of thirst. I clothe the sky with darkness and make sackcloth its covering.
Isaiah 50:2-3 (NIV)

Today's Truth:
Considering Who God is, there is no question that we should love and serve Him with our whole being.

Staggering:
bewildering
extraordinary

Prayer of Praise

Father, I so often forget that You are THE Mighty God. Nothing is bigger than You, nor does anyone put restrictions on You except Yourself. This fact fosters two significant reactions in my heart. First, I am humbled as I consider Your tremendous and inconceivable character. Secondly, I rejoice in knowing that You, the Great God, are my FATHER...a good, loving Lord. Amen.

Personal Meditation

...You will one day bring justice to all the nations.

My righteousness draws near speedily, my salvation is on the way, and my arm will bring justice to the nations. The islands will look to me and wait in hope for my arm.
Isaiah 51:5 (NIV)

Today's Truth:
God will uphold me with His righteous right arm.

Rule:
influence greatly

Prayer of Praise

Even without us knowing, Father, Your influence is dominant. You alone have the controlling power over all the nations in the world. I praise You for the direction You give us, even though we are not always aware of Your presence. My world is filled with unrest, wars and rumors of wars. How wonderful to know that Your salvation is approaching. It is deeply reassuring to know that people from all corners of the world will one day long for Your appearing. Amen.

Personal Meditation

...Your acts of deliverance are unending.

Look high in the skies and watch the earth beneath, for the skies shall disappear like smoke, the earth shall wear out like a garment and the people of the earth shall die like flies. But my salvation lasts forever; my righteous rule will never die nor end.
Isaiah 51:6 (LB)

Today's Truth:

For generations, God has pardoned sin because of Christ. He will continue restoring people to Himself until final judgment.

Salvation:
deliverance
pardon
restoration

Prayer of Praise

Everything in my world comes to an end, Father...everything has its life cycle:

> trees
> flowers
> birds of the air
> animals of the forest and fields
> humankind

But that is not true with You! How I praise You for giving me salvation that NEVER ends. It is so comforting to know that Your righteous reign will never cease. Amen.

Personal Meditation

...You raise me above all my fears.

I, even I, am he who comforts you. Who are you that you
fear mortal men, the sons of men, who are but grass.
Isaiah 51:12 (NIV)

Today's Truth:
God has the power to trade my fearful
spirit for confidence and a fresh outlook.

Comfort:
console
bring relief
support

Prayer of Praise

The way You quiet my fears and strengthen me is a marvelous thing,
Father. The comfort You offer Your people comes in such practical
ways: when I'm in a crisis, You bring comfort; when sorrow seems to
overwhelm, You give joy. One of the greatest comforts is that I don't
need to fear people, for they wither and pass away as does the grass
about me. BUT YOU, You are continuous…steadfast. Amen.

Personal Meditation

...You took up my sin and delivered me from its penalty.

Surely he took up our infirmities and carried our sorrows, yet we considered him stricken by God, smitten by him, and afflicted. But he was pierced for our transgressions, he was crushed for our iniquities; the punishment that brought us peace was upon him, and by his wounds we are healed.
Isaiah 53:4-5 (NIV)

Today's Truth:
Jesus paid the debt I couldn't pay. Now I have the honor of serving Him as Lord of my life!

Took up:
carried
assumed

Prayer of Praise

Father, my words cannot give You the praises due You for tackling the responsibility of all of my wrongdoing. You, the Creator of the heavens and earth, personally took my place for what I deserved. Thank You for giving me life! Please continue to heal me spiritually and deepen my understanding of Who You are. Show me today one way that I can better serve You. Amen.

Personal Meditation

...You, Jesus, lived a sinless life on earth.

He was assigned a grave with the wicked,
and with the rich in his death, though he had done no violence,
nor was any deceit in his mouth.
Isaiah 53:9 (NIV)

Today's Truth:
The One we serve is perfect.

Sinless:
blameless
exemplary
undefiled

Prayer of Praise

In spite of my sin wounding You, You overcame sin and death for me. You, Who could do no wrong, took every blow my sin could give and made a way to heaven for me. I understand that violent people often die for their acts of physical force against another, but You died with not one act against another. I give You praise for Your magnificent gift to me! Amen.

Personal Meditation

...You give strength to the humble.

The high and lofty one who inhabits eternity, the Holy One, says this:
I live in that high and holy place where those with contrite,
humble spirits dwell; and I refresh the humble
and give new courage to those with repentant hearts.
Isaiah 57:15 (LB)

Today's Truth:
God is eager to renew the spirit of those
who are sorry for their sin and turn from it.

Humble:
submissive
remorseful

Prayer of Praise

I give You glory, Lord, for refreshing me and picking me up when I
fall. Yet I have learned (and I read in Your Word) that a repentant heart
is what You need to see before You pick me up again. I am so glad that
You wait for this, Lord. It causes me to give evidence of not only my
sorrow but also of my choice to turn from my sin and focus again on
You. Amen.

Personal Meditation

...You love to help those who obey You.

Since ancient times no one has heard, no ear has perceived, no eye has seen
any God besides you, who acts on behalf of those who wait for him. You come
to the help of those who gladly do right, who remember your ways.
Isaiah 64:4-5a (NIV)

Today's Truth:

God delights in my following His
commands. I am on His side and He
supports me.

Remember:

keep
recall
observe

Prayer of Praise

How exciting to serve You, God; One who stands up for those who
honor Your headship and revere Your authority through doing what
You say. Yet, hand in hand with this statement, I praise You that You
are a forgiving God who does not leave us to our own abilities. You
faithfully offer help to Your children, forever look after us, and take
delight in who we are. Amen.

Personal Meditation

...You knew me before I was even conceived.

The Lord said to me, "I knew you before you were formed within your mother's womb; before you were born I sanctified you and appointed you as my spokesman to the world."
Jeremiah 1:4-5 (LB)

Today's Truth:
God designed me on purpose.

Knew:
understood
distinguished

Prayer of Praise

Before I was a twinkle in my father and mother's eyes, You, God, knew:

where I would be born.
who would bear me.
what I would do with my life.
when I would come home to heaven.

It is so easy to trust You, Father, because I know I am known by You in all ways. Even my words are known to You before I speak them. AMAZING!! Amen.

Personal Meditation

...You allow me to have an understanding of who You, my Maker, is.

"...but let him who boasts boast about this: that he understands and knows me, that I am the LORD, who exercises kindness, justice and righteousness on earth, for in these I delight," declares the LORD.
Jeremiah 9:24 (NIV)

Today's Truth:
Knowing the LORD is all that matters!

Knows:
discerns
experiences
recognizes

Prayer of Praise

Father, the above verse suggests so many attributes to praise You for:
    Your love is steadfast.
    You bring justice.
    You advocate righteousness.
    You truly know me.
    You love to be the God You are.
I will boast in You alone, Father. I celebrate Your deeds and great abilities and love to proclaim them to others. Amen.

Personal Meditation

...You deliver me from harm.

Sing to the LORD! Give praise to the LORD! He rescues
the life of the needy from the hands of the wicked.
Jeremiah 20:13 (NIV)

Today's Truth:

The Lord clears away all that is too
much for us to handle, so that when we
come through, the path is just right.

Rescue:
free
preserve
recover

Prayer of Praise

I do give You praise, Father, because You care so much for those in
need. It doesn't seem to matter what the need is, because You provide
a way out. You especially care for us when anyone wants to harm us.
How easy it is then to rest in Your constant care. Amen.

Personal Meditation

...You offer me relief from emotional and physical wear.

For I have given rest to the weary and joy to all the sorrowing.
Jeremiah 31:25 (LB)

Today's Truth:
God gives us just what we need.

Rest:
relief
peace
revivification

Prayer of Praise

Father, often I have seen in Your children the joy You give in the midst of sorrow and suffering. You cause us to not allow our circumstances to dictate our joy. You alone are the giver of joy! Your Word says that You have already given rest and joy as I need it. Your supply is never used up! Amen.

Personal Meditation

...You can do all things.

*O Lord God! You have made the heavens and earth
by your great power; nothing is too hard for you!
Jeremiah 32:17 (LB)*

Today's Truth:
There is nothing that is beyond God.
And yet He does not act impulsively,
but rather, intentionally.

Hard:
burdensome
formidable
rigorous

Prayer of Praise

Father, the word NOTHING is an amazing word: NOTHING... NO,
NOT ONE THING... is too hard for You! The burdens and needs You
know about and see are not too difficult for You. You are able to carry
all my cares and have wonderful answers for them as well. If I could
see and know just a tiny portion of what You assess every day, after the
first few seconds, I'd crash...BUT NOT YOU! You oversee all things
and can overcome anything. Amen.

Personal Meditation

...You are the God of the supernatural.

You have done incredible things in the land of Egypt—things still remembered to this day. And you have continued to do great miracles in Israel and all around the world. You have made your name very great, as it is today.
Jeremiah 32:20 (LB)

Today's Truth:
God's mighty acts are
recognized around the world.

Incredible:
extraordinary
astonishing
glorious

Prayer of Praise

Father, it's so exciting that You are at work among the nations.
All around the world, even at this very moment, You are doing
extraordinary things. Your name is truly great, and one day all people
will bow before You. I praise You most of all today for making a way
for me to have everlasting life. It is the greatest of all miracles! Amen.

Personal Meditation

...You are answerable to no one.

For who is like me and who can call me to account?
Jeremiah 49:19c (LB)

Today's Truth:
God is held accountable only by
Himself. He is also perfectly good.

Account:
reckoning
hold responsible
monitor

Prayer of Praise

How I praise You, Father God, that You are the authority in my life and
are over my life. What comfort there is to know that my God... the God
above all the gods of humankind, is not answerable to anyone! You are
perfect in all Your ways. One day, when I have my special appointment
with You, I will give You an accounting for my life. Oh, teach me to
number my days, and apply my life with wisdom. Amen.

Personal Meditation

...You select the world's leaders.

...at last he knew that the Most High overrules the kingdoms of men,
and that he appoints anyone he desires to reign over them.
Daniel 5:21b (LB)

Today's Truth:
God determines who rules a nation.

Appoint:
decree
ordain

Prayer of Praise

You raise up leaders... You bring them down... none can be in
opposition to You. Though they deliberately seem to be so, all these
things regarding leaders, Father, can only be done by You, the Lord of
hosts, the great I AM! In so many nations around me there is discord,
war, famine and civil uprising. How comforting to know that when
there is unrest and when there are problems on every side—YOU ARE
ALYWAYS IN CHARGE! Amen.

Personal Meditation

...Your reign will never cease.

Then King Darius wrote to all the peoples, nations and men of every language throughout the land: "May you prosper greatly! I issue a decree that in every part of my kingdom people must fear and reverence the God of Daniel. For he is the living God and he endures forever; his kingdom will not be destroyed, his dominion will never end."
Daniel 6:25-26 (NIV)

Today's Truth:
God, nor his works, will
ever come to an end.

Reverence:
adore
exalt
worship

Prayer of Praise

Father, my world is always changing, but You NEVER CHANGE! How incredible! You are so constant and consistent, so strong and enduring! From the time of Daniel, and even before, Your kingdom is always the same, and You will always be powerful. Oh, may I also "tremble and fear" before You, in the truest sense of worship and adoration. Amen.

Personal Meditation

...You promise and keep Your Word.

I prayed to the LORD my God and confessed: "O Lord, the great and awesome God, who keeps his covenant of love with all who love him and obey his commands, we have sinned and done wrong.'"
Daniel 9:4-5a (NIV)

Today's Truth:
God keeps His Word.

Covenant:
oath
commitment
promise

Prayer of Praise

How amazing that You have never broken Your covenants, nor ever will. Your promise to be compassionate and show me kindness (just one of many promises) is always constant as I grow to love You more through reading Your precious Word! How many times I have experienced the fulfillment of Your pledges to me. You deserve all my praise and all my worship. Amen.

Personal Meditation

...You give me grace, even when I have resisted Your authority.

*The Lord our God is merciful and forgiving, even
though we have rebelled against him.*
Daniel 9:9 (NIV)

Today's Truth:
God gives many chances for people
to come to Him.

Rebel:
defy
disobey
oppose

Prayer of Praise

Father, there have been times I have resisted Your control and have
rebelled against You, BUT PRAISE THE LORD—You are full of
love; in mercy You pardon my rebellion and sin. Thank You for Your
forgiveness. It is a beautiful thing! May I never use this truth about
Your character as an excuse to not be right with You at all times. Amen.

Personal Meditation

...You have redeemed my soul and offer eternal life.

Create in me a pure heart, O God, and renew a
steadfast spirit within me.
Psalm 51:10 (NIV)

Today's Truth:
God purifies our hearts and makes our
faith firm within us.

Steadfast:
firm
stable
constant

Prayer of Praise

Sometimes, Father, my priorities are all mixed up. My thoughts are centered around myself and my needs. Please clear my heart and make my spirit a rich soul, that the Words of Life I read become seeds of new thoughts. Help them take root and grow in me a strong, vibrant and beautiful faith. Amen.

Personal Meditation

...You do incredibly unusual things!

And the LORD commanded the fish,
and it vomited Jonah onto dry land.
Jonah 2:10 (NIV)

Today's Truth:
God truly does work in
mysterious ways.

Commanded:
directed
ordered
willed

Prayer of Praise

Amazing! You commanded the great fish to spit out Jonah– and it did!
Father, indeed You know how to get our attention. A fish? Swallowing
Jonah? Yet he lived to do Your will. He was horrified, Father! How he
cried out for mercy! Did he fly through the air when the fish spit him
out? How did You keep him from being fish food? Three days and
three nights inside the fish... My only reply is that You are an amazing,
incredible God. Only You could orchestrate such a thing! May we, in
our so-called human sophistication and our very limited knowledge,
not doubt Your Word. Amen.

Personal Meditation

...You don't allow unnecessary harm or pain.

And when God saw that they had put a stop to their evil ways, he abandoned his plan to destroy them, and didn't carry it through.
Jonah 3:10 (LB)

Today's Truth:
God's anger lasts but a moment; His favor lasts a lifetime.

Abandoned:
gave up
discarded

Prayer of Praise

How easy to praise You, dear Father, for
    loving me,
    being slow to anger,
    being filled with justice,
    showing mercy.
The moment I turn away from my sin, You are immediately willing to abundantly pardon and forgive me. You are merciful and kind. Amen.

Personal Meditation

...You are protective of Your children.

The LORD is a jealous and avenging God;
the LORD takes vengeance and is filled with wrath.
The LORD takes vengeance on his foes
and maintains his wrath against his enemies.
Nahum 1:2 (NIV)

Today's Truth:
God is not a pushover; He brings judgment.

Jealous:
protective
zealous

Prayer of Praise

I praise You because all nature is at Your command. You...
    show Your power in the cyclone,
    show Your power in the raging storms,
    cause rivers and oceans to become dry sand,
    cause lush pastures to fade away and green forests to wilt,
    make mountains quake and hills to melt.
When enemies come against Your children who walk in obedience to
You, Your fierceness is like fire toward those who would harm them.
Amen.

Personal Meditation

...When I have a need, You are the One to Whom I can turn.

The Lord is good. When trouble comes, he is the place
to go! And he knows everyone who trusts in him!
Nahum 1:7 (LB)

Today's Truth:

God's answer and direction is sufficient for
my every question and need.

Trouble:
difficulty
disorder
suffering

Prayer of Praise

Father, how often in the course of this day will I find You to be my
hiding place, my rest stop, the place to go. When I need Your comfort
and the wonderful sense of Your presence, I know You will surround
me and protect me. You are good and so trustworthy. You always meet
with me in the sanctuary of my heart. Amen.

Personal Meditation

...As You cared for Jerusalem—
You even more so care for me.

"And I myself will be a wall of fire around it," declares the LORD,
"and I will be its glory within."
Zechariah 2:5 (NIV)

Today's Truth:
God will manage and care for all my
life's issues if I let Him.

Glory:
exaltation
splendor

Prayer of Praise

Lord, it is so good to have You as my Heavenly Father. You have made
my job so simple—I just need to trust in You. Yet, doing this can be
hard at times. But You have given me Your Scriptures to read as a
testimony of how You have acted throughout history. Reading about
Your many mighty acts gives me assurance that I want to put total faith
in You. I praise You that You are a good God and are capable of dealing
with all my concerns. Amen.

Personal Meditation

...You are the King!

Rejoice greatly, O Daughter of Zion! Shout, Daughter of Jerusalem!
See, your king comes to you, righteous and having salvation, gentle
and riding on a donkey, on a colt, the foal of a donkey.
Zechariah 9:9 (NIV)

Today's Truth:
Jesus is the best kind of Ruler—perfect, kind,
able to save...

Rejoice:
celebrate
revel
be overjoyed

Prayer of Praise

Jesus, it is said that You came to proclaim peace to the nations. I
know that no one, Lord, can disarm the unruly nations but You! You
alone hold the keys to every world situation. When things seem out of
control, with You they are always in control. Praise be to the Victor—
the returning King of Kings. You alone will disarm the entire world
and usher in true peace. Amen.

Personal Meditation

...Your people are always on Your heart.

Come to the place of safety, all you prisoners, for there is yet hope! I promise right now, I will repay you two mercies for each of your woes!
Zechariah 9:12 (LB)

Today's Truth:
God upholds His children.

Repay:
compensate

Prayer of Praise

There is never a day, Father, that someone does not come against Your beloved people. Praise be to You alone for going ahead of us and doubling Your mercies for each of our heartaches. Terrorism is a daily event in our world, but though we have heartaches, Your mercies refresh us continuously. Amen.

Personal Meditation

...You, Father God, find such pleasure in Your beloved Son!

*And a voice from heaven said, "This is my Son,
whom I love; with him I am well pleased."
Matthew 3:17 (NIV)*

Today's Truth:
God delights in His Son, and takes
delight in me!

Pleasure:
joy
fruition

Prayer of Praise

Father, when I am pleased in my children and they bring me joy, I am reminded that Your Son, Jesus, also brings You great pleasure. How perfect in oneness You are. One in thought, one in purpose, one in goals. No wonder You are well-pleased in Him—Christ, Your Beloved Son! Amen.

Personal Meditation

...You reach out to people.

Jesus went throughout Galilee, teaching in their synagogues,
preaching the good news of the kingdom, and healing every
disease and sickness among the people.
Matthew 4:23 (NIV)

Today's Truth:

Jesus holds forth His open arms to me,
patiently waiting for me to run
to His embrace.

Reach out:
relate
love
minister

Prayer of Praise

Oh, Father, how eager You are to permeate my world with Your Good News. You have the most beautiful, perfect heart. I praise You for always being the Teacher Who brightens my way as You teach me every day more of Who You are. I praise You for preserving the Bible all these centuries, as it is my manual for life. Amen.

Personal Meditation

...You heal those broken in body and heart, soul and spirit.

News about him spread all over Syria, and people brought to him all who were ill with various diseases, those suffering severe pain, the demonpossessed, those having seizures, and the paralyzed, and he healed them.
Matthew 4:23-24 (NIV)

Today's Truth:
God brings to me His healing hand.

Healed:
restored
made whole
regenerated

Prayer of Praise

How often I have witnessed Your healing power, Heavenly Father!
    You have made people well again as it has been in Your will.
    You have restored soundness of mind.
    You have made people free from deep grief and sorrow.
    You have brought spiritual healing as we invited You to be
        our Savior and Lord.
All because You are the Great Physician, the One Who created me and
gives me life and breath each day. Amen.

Personal Meditation

...You are a giver of good gifts.

And if you hardhearted, sinful men know how to give good gifts to your children, won't your Father in heaven even more certainly give good gifts to those who ask him for them?
Matthew 7:11 (LB)

Today's Truth:
As I follow Christ, I receive countless blessings from above.

Giver:
bestower
benefactor

Prayer of Praise

I praise You, Lord, that when I am disobeying You, You sometimes choose to withhold Your good gifts to me. This keeps me mindful of my actions and thoughts and catches my attention to examine myself and see what I am missing. Yet at other times, You don't withhold Your blessing, and I receive good gifts even when I am in the wrong. I glorify You for being a God Who, despite the status or consistency of my obedience, never stops loving me! Amen.

Personal Meditation

...Your Holy Spirit expresses Your thoughts through Your children.

For it won't be you doing the talking—it will be the
Spirit of your heavenly Father speaking through you!
Matthew 10:20 (LB)

Today's Truth:
The Holy Spirit knows I need His help as
I try to communicate God's Truth—He is
quick to come to my aid.

Express:
convey
disclose
impart

Prayer of Praise

In every circumstance where I long to share my faith, I praise You for
the thoughts You put into my mind that will draw people to You. You
are the Great In-Gatherer, the Lord of the Harvest. All around me are
those You have prepared and are preparing to know You. I praise You
that if I listen closely and seek an answer, Your Spirit never fails to
reveal to me what I should say and do. Amen.

Personal Meditation

...You, Jesus Christ, are the Father's Chosen One.

This was to fulfill what was spoken through the prophet Isaiah: "Here is my servant whom I have chosen, the one I love, in whom I delight; I will put my Spirit on him, and he will proclaim justice to the nations."
Matthew 12:17-18 (NIV)

Today's Truth:

As God gave Christ His Spirit to accomplish His purpose on Earth, God also has given the Holy Spirit to me to do the same.

Chosen:
selected
appointed

Prayer of Praise

No one is worthy of praise as are You, Jesus!
   You will judge the nations.
   You do not crush the weak.
   You do not quench the smallest hope.
   You will end all conflict with Your final victory.
                                   Amen.

Personal Meditation

...Your Name—LORD JESUS CHRIST—shall be the hope of all the world.

In his name the nations will put their hope.
Matthew 12:21 (NIV)

Today's Truth:
I can rest assured that Jesus will prevail over evil.

Hope:
expectation
confidence

Prayer of Praise

You alone give HOPE!
    Happiness
    Overcoming power
    Pardon
    Everlasting life
HOPE for all the world! Every nation, every people group, and every tongue. Amen.

Personal Meditation

...You fed over 30,000 people from five loaves of bread and two fish!

Then he told the people to sit down on the grass; and he took the five loaves and two fish, looked up into the sky and asked God's blessing on the meal, then broke the loaves apart and gave them to the disciples to place before the people. And everyone ate until full!
Matthew 14:19-20a (LB)

Today's Truth:
God works miracles in my life.

Blessing:
favor
support

Prayer of Praise

Whatever You do, You do with all Your might! When everyone had eaten ALL they wanted, TWELVE BASKETS WERE LEFT OVER! Not only were twelve baskets left over, but each was filled to the top! I long to have been there that day! What must that have been like to see a small loaf of bread keep breaking off pieces for another to eat, then another, and another? I find no word in my human vocabulary to adequately praise You! Amen.

Personal Meditation

...You allow the miraculous.

Then Peter called to him: "Sir, if it is really you, tell me to come over to you, walking on the water." "All right," the Lord said, "come along!" So Peter went over the side of the boat and walked on the water toward Jesus.
Matthew 14:28-29 (LB)

Today's Truth:
As we move closer to God– He lifts us above all that concerns us.

Come:
draw nearer

Prayer of Praise

Father, miracles are where You are. It was by Your Word that Peter's faith was deepened. It deepened enough for him to reach out, to move toward You. And that is where he saw You work miracles. Today, as I read Your Word, Your Holy Spirit calls to me. It calls me to move closer to You and not to stand here waiting for Your hand to move in my life. I will pursue You, and, in doing so, I will see You work miracles in my circumstances. Help me, Lord, to be faithful. Amen.

Personal Meditation

…Jesus, You are the Son of God.

"But what about you?" he asked. "Who do you say I am?"
Simon Peter answered, "You are the Christ, the Son of the living God."
Matthew 16:16 (NIV)

Today's Truth:

Everyone must acknowledge for himself/herself… Who is the Christ?

Christ:
Messiah

Prayer of Praise

Father, You asked of Peter who he said You were. You are still asking this today from each of us. You compel a response from us. I acknowledge and confess that You are my Christ, my Redeemer, and my Messiah. Amen.

Personal Meditation

...all goodness lives in You, Lord.

"When you call me good you are calling me God,"
Jesus replied, "for God alone is truly good."
Matthew 19:17a (LB)

Today's Truth:
God alone is truly good!

Truly:
with accuracy

Prayer of Praise

Father, in my life, produce the moral excellence and kindness that is characteristic of Your goodness. Your goodness is a fruit of the Holy Spirit. May Your goodness touch all I touch today. It is true that only You, God, are absolutely good. Amen.

Personal Meditation

...You are the Giver of eternal life.

This remark confounded the disciples "Then who in the world can be saved?" they asked. Jesus looked at them intently and said, "Humanly speaking, no one. But with God, everything is possible."
Matthew 19:23-26 (LB)

Today's Truth:
In God's goodness He has made salvation open to all who believe.

Confounded:
perplexed

Prayer of Praise

How I praise You for receiving me into Your family. Yes, Father, I thank You that it is possible for You to give eternal life to those of us who come asking to be saved. To realize that I am in Your family is incredible! Amen.

Personal Meditation

...One day You will return.

*...Men of Galilee, why are you standing here staring
at the sky? Jesus has gone away to heaven,
and some day, just as he went, he will return!
Acts 1:11 (LB)*

Today's Truth:
God will return in all glory,
power, and majesty.

Return:
recur
come back

Prayer of Praise

I watch the clouds, Lord Jesus, in anticipation of Your glorious return.
You have promised that one day... the day You have planned from the
foundations of the world...You will return to take us home to be with
You forever and ever. Until that day, Lord, keep me faithful to the work
You have planned for me, that others may share in anticipation of You.
Amen.

Personal Meditation

...You are God to those in every generation who know You as Savior.

Don't you realize that God was speaking directly to you when he said,
"I am the God of Abraham, Isaac, and Jacob"?
So God is not the God of the dead, but of the living.
Matthew 22:31b-32 (LB)

Today's Truth:
The God of Abraham, Isaac, and Jacob
is the God of all who believe.

Living:
active
still used

Prayer of Praise

God, as I read the accounts of the lives of Abraham, Isaac, and Jacob,
I am made aware of the lives of flawed men, but men who desired a
change in their lives and to lead lives in obedience to You. It is in their
footsteps that I walk and desire to truly live as You would have me to
live– to be counted among the Living. Amen.

Personal Meditation

...Your words endure forever.

Heaven and earth will pass away,
but my words will never pass away.
Matthew 24:35 (NIV)

Today's Truth:
Upon the unending truth
of Your Word I shall stand!

Forever:
always
in perpetuity

Prayer of Praise

It is reassuring to know that the Truth of Your Word remains forever.
How glorious it is to think that the principles and truths that You have
laid before us in Your Word for us to build our lives upon will outlast
even the earth itself. Thank You, God, for the confidence we can have
in the Scriptures. Amen.

Personal Meditation

...You rose from the dead and You are alive today.

*The angel said to the women, "Do not be afraid,
for I know that you are looking for Jesus, who was
crucified. He is not here; he has risen, just as he said.
Come and see the place where he lay."
Matthew 28:5-6 (NIV)*

Today's Truth:
Jesus Christ has risen. We serve a risen Lord!

Risen:
lives again

Prayer of Praise

Two thousand years after Your resurrection we stand amazed! The tomb is empty, and You have conquered death and the grave. Victory is Yours! Because of You, we no longer need to be afraid; the sting of death is gone. We serve the one and only risen Savior. Amen.

Personal Meditation

…You, Jesus, have been given the right to command all of heaven and earth.

He told his disciples, "I have been given all authority in heaven and earth…"
Matthew 28:18 (LB)

" …and be sure of this—that I am with you always, even to the end of the world."
Matthew 28:20b (LB)

Today's Truth:
All authority in heaven and earth is in the hands of a loving God.

Authority:
personal power

Prayer of Praise

Jesus, in You I rest. Your authority is never ending. You alone have jurisdiction throughout the universe. Who can compare with You? You are always supreme and always in control. Nothing in heaven or on earth happens without Your knowledge and consent. Amen.

Personal Meditation

...You are greater than anyone who has lived or ever will live!

In the book written by the prophet Isaiah, God announced that he would send his Son to earth, and that a special messenger would arrive first to prepare the world for his coming. —Mark 1:2 (LB)

This messenger was John the Baptist. —Mark 1:4a (LB)

"Here is a sample of his preaching: 'Someone is coming soon who is far greater than I am, so much greater that I am not even worthy to be his slave." —Mark 1:7 (LB)

Today's Truth
The God of all-surpassing greatness shall be praised.

Greater:
superior

Prayer of Praise

Father, as I enter Your presence, I am made aware of the awesomeness of Your glory. There is none equal to You. Yet it is Your desire to have fellowship with us. There is none that can compare with You. Amen.

Personal Meditation

...You call me to hold to the course and tell others about You.

Jesus called out to them, "Come, follow me!
And I will make you fishermen for the souls of men!"
Mark 1:17 (LB)

Today's Truth:
Our purpose is found in following the God of all creation.

Follow:
be under leadership

Prayer of Praise

God, I need Your leadership. You call out to me... I hear Your voice and am compelled to follow You. Your invitation, however, is not just to follow in word, but in deed. Lord, Your way–the steps that You have taken–are steps of love that I must follow; steps of love, sacrifice and compassion. Lord, lead on. Amen

Personal Meditation

...You read my mind.

Jesus could read their minds...
Mark 2:8a (LB)

Today's Truth:
Nothing is hidden from God.

Mind Reader:
one who knows another's thoughts

Prayer of Praise

You alone know my thoughts. Yes, even the hidden, secret thoughts that lie buried in my mind are not hidden from You! Purify my mind that I may praise You perfectly. Give me the mind of Christ. Amen.

Personal Meditation

Day 271

...In the midst of many opinions, I can trust You.

But Jesus ignored their comments and said to
Jairus, "Don't be afraid. Just trust me."
Mark 5:36 (LB)

Today's Truth:
Trust and obedience to God
will cast out fear and doubt.

Trust:
to have confidence in

Prayer of Praise

Today I trust You to do what is best for me as Your child. I trust You
because You knew me before I was born. I trust You because You know
me today. Even while others may instill doubt and fear, as I listen to
and rely upon You, they are quieted. You have called me to depend on
You. You have told me to not be afraid. In You I will trust. Amen.

Personal Meditation

...I only see You, Jesus!

Then a cloud appeared and enveloped them, and a voice came from the cloud:
"This is my Son, whom I love. Listen to him!" Suddenly, when they looked
around, they no longer saw anyone with them except Jesus.
Mark 9:7-8 (NIV)

Today's Truth:
The presence of God will change our focus.

See:
witness
experience firsthand.

Prayer of Praise

I want to see You, Jesus, daily working in and through my life. When
I look upon You, everything that does not reflect You is diminished. I
desire Your presence. In Your presence my emotions are quieted. In
Your presence I am comforted. In Your presence my fears subside. In
Your presence I am changed. Amen.

Personal Meditation

...You love children.

Once when some mothers were bringing their children to Jesus to bless them, the disciples shooed them away, telling them not to bother him. But when Jesus saw what was happening he was very much displeased with his disciples and said to them, "Let the children come to me, for the Kingdom of God belongs to such as they. Don't send them away!"
Mark 10:13-14 (LB)

Today's Truth:
God created children to be a model of faith.

Bless:
guard
protect

Prayer of Praise

I am moved by Your heart for the children. It is a joy to watch the lives of these little ones: their passion is infectious; their trust is complete; their joy is overwhelming. Father, they model for me the person You will me to be... Your child. Amen.

Personal Meditation

...Your Word is timeless.

The grass withers and the flowers fall,
but the word of our God stands forever.
Isaiah 40:8 (NIV)

Today's Truth:

The Bible speaks Truth today,
just as it did at the time it was
recorded.

Timeless:
eternal
unchanging
unfailing

Prayer of Praise

Oh, how I praise You, Father, for giving me the enduring Word... a
Holy Book that shows me Your character and mighty acts, and goes on
for all time. The Scriptures impart in me knowledge of the past, offer
insight for the present, and tell of coming events of the future. Give
me a great hunger to read Your Word so I will have spiritual life and
health. Your Word is eternal, so allow it to take eternal root in my soul.
Amen.

Personal Meditation

...You will come back to take Your children home.

"Then all mankind will see me, the Messiah, coming in the clouds with great power and glory. And I will send out the angels to gather together my chosen ones from all over the world—from the farthest bounds of earth and heaven."
Mark 13:26-27 (LB)

Today's Truth:

Christ will one day gather up all those who have truly made Him LORD of their life.

Chosen:
those saved by God

Prayer of Praise

I saw a brilliant opening in a cloud, Jesus, and through it streamed rays of light. As I said to You at that moment, so now I do pen, "Come soon, Lord Jesus!" One day You will appear in the heavens with Your angels, and come in great power and glory. What will that be like? From every corner of the world, Your chosen will rise to meet You. Amen.

Personal Meditation

...What You say stands forever.

Heaven and earth will pass away, but my
words will never pass away.
Mark 13:31 (NIV)

Today's Truth:
We can be sure that what God says
will happen, will happen and what
He promises to do, He will do.

Stand:
endure successfully
remain

Prayer of Praise

In everything You say, Your promises will always be fulfilled. You are
sure to remain merciful, just, and in pursuit of a righteous people.
Your standards are never lowered, and Your love is never less than
total. The salvation You provided me through Jesus' death, burial and
resurrection will one day be complete. Yes, Your Word will continue on
into heaven—it will NEVER PASS AWAY! Amen.

Personal Meditation

...You, Jesus, are the very Son of God.

But the angel said to her, "Do not be afraid, Mary, you have found favor with God. You will be with child and give birth to a son, and you are to give him the name Jesus. He will be great and will be called the Son of the Most High. The Lord God will give him the throne of his father David, and he will reign over the house of Jacob forever; his kingdom will never end."
Luke 1:30-33 (NIV)

Today's Truth:
Jesus, the Son of God, entirely God Himself, humbled Himself and came to earth for us.

Great:
exalted
superior

Prayer of Praise

I stand quietly in worship, knowing that You are the Greatest, the very Son of God, whose reign will never come to an end! What an announcement You gave to Mary! Did her heart and mind race in disbelief, or did she immediately know the excitement the proclamation brought? It is hardly conceivable that You, Lord of all, came into this world to love Your people, teach them how to live, and ultimately save them. Thank You for Your sacrifice, Jesus. Amen.

Personal Meditation

...In You, all things are possible.

For nothing is impossible with God.
Luke 1:37 (NIV)

Today's Truth:
With Christ in us, we have access
to God's incredible power.

Impossible:
incapable of occurring
hopeless

Prayer of Praise

Oh, Holy Jesus, I praise You because You are able to make every
promise in Your Word possible, and You will be faithful to bring them
to pass. I especially look forward to Your promise that I will one day
see You face to face. What a wonderful thing to be connected to the
God through Whom everything is possible! Amen.

Personal Meditation

...You show forgiveness to each generation.

His mercy goes on from generation to generation,
to all who reverence him.
Luke 1:50 (LB)

Today's Truth:
God does not stop showing favor
through the ages.

Mercy:
compassion
grace
blessing

Prayer of Praise

Yes, from one generation to the next, and still on to the next, Your compassion and mercy toward us never ends! When my generation is gone, Your mercy goes on. When that generation is gone, Your forgiveness still does not cease. Your precious favor and touch will bless every generation until time is no more. Amen.

Personal Meditation

Day 280

...You lift up the needy.

He has torn princes from their thrones and
exalted the lowly. He has satisfied the hungry
hearts and sent the rich away with empty hands.
Luke 1:52-53 (LB)

Today's Truth:
God is near to the brokenhearted and is
an ever-present help in time of need.

Lowly:
humble
low in position

Prayer of Praise

How well I know and remember that even before I knew You, You fed
me. Even before I acknowledged You as Lord, You clothed me. I am
fully satisfied in You, dear Savior! Those years of being on the street
and of knowing hunger one day came to an end, and You satisfied the
hunger of my heart! You filled me with Yourself, and the days of fear
and dread You took away. Amen.

Personal Meditation

...You remember Your commitment to those who seek and serve You.

And how he has helped his servant Israel! He has not forgotten his promise to be merciful.
Luke 1:54 (LB)

Today's Truth:
God will never forget to be merciful to His children.

Remember:
retain forever
act upon
follow through with

Prayer of Praise

Father, what love You have for Your own. I may be battered, but not broken, bruised by my enemies, but never conquered. Your promise to never forget me has proven true over and over. Amen.

Personal Meditation

...You are the Light of the world.

He is the Light that will shine upon the nations, and
he will be the glory of your people Israel!
Luke 2:32 (LB)

Today's Truth:
Truth and love radiates from
the Light of the world.

Shine:
be preeminent
give light
radiate

Prayer of Praise

No nation is too small or any people group insignificant to You! You
are the Light that is beaming upon them—You, Jesus, the Father's
anointed King! I praise You that Your light teaches us what is right and
illuminates what it is that You desire from us. Your light reaches to the
remotest corners of the world. May You always be worshipped by every
tongue, every tribe and every nation. Amen.

Personal Meditation

...You are the Father's beloved Son.

When all the people were being baptized, Jesus was baptized too.
And as he was praying, heaven was opened and the Holy Spirit
descended on him in bodily form like a dove. And a voice came from
heaven: "You are my Son, whom I love; with you I am well pleased."
Luke 3:21-22 (NIV)

Today's Truth:
Christ is worthy of my love and praise.

Beloved:
cherished
worshiped
prized

Prayer of Praise

Father, today I give You honor and all praise for sending Your much-loved Son to Earth. I will never know the depth of Your agony when Jesus literally became my sin. What a price He paid; what an example He set! He overcame every temptation and defeated death, sin, and Satan. Hallelujah! Amen.

Personal Meditation

...You are able to do miraculous deeds.

They got up, drove him out of the town, and took him to the brow of the hill on which the town was built, in order to throw him down the cliff. But he walked right through the crowd and went on his way.
Luke 4:29-30 (NIV)

Today's Truth:
There are no limitations or predicaments for God.

Through:
from one end to the other
unhindered

Prayer of Praise

Jesus, here are the religious leaders taking You by the arm to throw You off the cliff, and suddenly, with ease, You move through the people, away from the cliff, and go on Your way...what a statement! No one can touch You without Your permission! You are able to prevail and have victory in all situations! Amen.

Personal Meditation

...While on earth, Jesus, You stayed connected to Your lifeline.

But he often withdrew to the wilderness for prayer.
Luke 5:16 (LB)

Today's Truth:
Prayer is the essence of
staying in touch with God.

Prayer:
communion
adoration
appeal

Prayer of Praise

Jesus, I am so thankful that You demonstrated perfectly what
an intimate relationship with the Father looks like—one full of
communion and communication. I praise You for setting such an
excellent example and for teaching Your children to be a people of
prayer. I also rejoice in the fact that though Satan accuses me before
You, the Holy Spirit stands in the gap for me. Amen.

Personal Meditation

Day 286

...You are aware of everything I am thinking.

How well he knew their thoughts!
Luke 6:8a (LB)

Today's Truth:

We conceal nothing from God.
No mask we may wear fools Him.

Thoughts:
ideas
opinions
judgements

Prayer of Praise

The fact that You know all my thoughts may not seem like a pleasant thing to praise You for, Father, but it really is amazing. There is no other with the ability to know my thoughts completely, as You do. Nothing in my mind is hidden from You. And besides knowing my every thought, Your Word also tells me that "You know what I am going to say before I even say it" (Psalm 139:4 LB). May my thoughts and my words be honoring to You. Amen.

Personal Meditation

...You even show kindness to those who are not grateful.

Love your enemies! Do good to them! Lend to them! And don't be concerned about the fact that they won't repay. Then your reward from heaven will be very great, and you will truly be acting as sons of God: for he is kind to the unthankful and to those who are very wicked.
Luke 6:35 (LB)

Today's Truth:

God's love is unconditional, and He calls us to love in the same way.

Unthankful:
unappreciative
self-centered
dissatisfied

Prayer of Praise

Father, I am amazed at the breadth of Your kindness. For me, it was while I was yet a sinner. How I praise You for not giving to me what my sin deserved, but rather You showed kindness beyond measure. Help me to have a similar attitude of love toward all those around me, the grateful and ungrateful alike. Amen.

Personal Meditation

...You are the Messiah.

*Then he asked them, "Who do you think I am?" Peter
replied, "The Messiah—the Christ of God!"
Luke 9:20 (LB)*

Today's Truth:
Jesus is God's chosen vessel to
save man, and He is God Himself.

Messiah:
Anointed One
Savior

Prayer of Praise

What matchless names You have, dear Jesus—one of which is
Messiah, the Christ of God! No name in this earth means so much to
me! I have learned in my walk with You that Your name holds great
power and utmost authority. Yes, it is truly the matchless name of
JESUS. Amen.

Personal Meditation

...You have sent us out to preach Your Word and Truth.

These were his instructions to them: "Plead with the Lord of the harvest to send out more laborers to help you, for the harvest is so plentiful and the workers so few."
Luke 10:2 (LB)

Today's Truth:

Many are thirsty for Christ. We need to give them Living Water to drink.

Harvest:
fruition
gathering
yield

Prayer of Praise

You so desire that I not only talk to You, but that I earnestly plead with You to send out more people to proclaim Your mighty acts and share Truth with others so people will feel remorse and sorrow for their sin and repent. This must happen if they are going to be able to acknowledge You as Lord! Give me courage to tell others about Your commandments and Your love so they may be part of the harvest that is gathered for You. Amen.

Personal Meditation

...You move people to repent.

But Zacchaeus stood up and said to the Lord, "Look, Lord! Here and now I give half of my possessions to the poor, and if I have cheated anybody out of anything, I will pay back four times the amount." Jesus said to him, "Today salvation has come to this house..."
Luke 19:8-9a (NIV)

Today's Truth:
The Holy Spirit and the Scriptures help us see our sin for what it is and learn how to live in God-honoring ways.

Repent:
lament
turn from
ask forgiveness

Prayer of Praise

All around me, Father, are dear people who need You as their Savior. I praise You for Your loving heart that calls the lost to feel sorrow for their sins. Just as You called Zacchaeus to come down quickly because You were bringing salvation to his home that day, so today, use me to help others to find You as their saving Lord. Amen.

Personal Meditation

...Your words are Truth itself.

*...for he was a hero to the people—they
hung on every word he said.*
Luke 19:48b (LB)

Today's Truth:
In God and His Word—I find Life.

Hero:
person of great courage
exemplar

Prayer of Praise

Great Savior, how I love You. What a day when I see You, and behold
You in all Your glory and splendor. Truly, my life is in You, Lord! Yes,
what a day that will be when my Jesus I shall see! Amen.

Personal Meditation

...You, Jesus, have always been.

*Before anything else existed, there was Christ, with
God. He has always been alive and is himself God.*
John 1:1-2 (LB)

Today's Truth:
God was, is, and is to come.

Exist:
live
be

Prayer of Praise

I wonder what Your existence was like before Creation? What was it
like when angels came into being, or when You formed other galaxies,
planets, and maybe even life forms beyond this earth? It is a mind-
boggling thing—unfathomable, actually—to try to think of how it is
possible that You have always existed. You had no beginning. I stand in
awe of You. Amen.

Personal Meditation

...You brought everything into existence.

Through him all things were made; without him nothing was made that has been made.
John 1:3 (NIV)

Today's Truth:
God longs for everything He made to know Him, their Maker, and bring glory to Him.

Create:
form
conceive
fashion

Prayer of Praise

Everything... yes, everything was made by Your hand!
Halibut fish
Hailstones
Hydrangea bushes
Humans
Father, You not only gave us life, but You created life for us to enjoy.
You've given us Your life... everlasting life! Amen.

Personal Meditation

...You offer me forgiveness.

*For Moses gave us only the Law with its rigid demands
and merciless justice, while Jesus Christ brought us loving
forgiveness as well.*
John 1:17 (LB)

Today's Truth:
Through Christ I am redeemed
and reconciled to God.

Forgiveness:
pardon
remission
mercy

Prayer of Praise

The greatest miracle of all is that when You became my Savior, Your
Word says that You put my sins into the deepest sea, never to be seen
again! Your Word also says that they are as far away as the east is
from the west, never to be remembered any more. What complete
forgiveness You give! Thank You for having such grace when I come to
You with a repentant heart. Amen.

Personal Meditation

...You died for all people.

For God so loved the world that he gave his one and only Son, that whoever believes in him shall not perish but have eternal life.
John 3:16 (NIV)

Today's Truth:
God is ready to save ALL who believe in Jesus. "Belief" infers submission to Christ and an attempt to heed His ways.

Believe:
trust
regard
affirm

Prayer of Praise

I am so grateful that "the world" means that all may come to You, Jesus—"whoever" includes ME! Even yet today, those who do not know You as their Savior may come to submit to You. How amazing that the door to salvation remains open. In the remotest corner of the world and to the most populated city, those who believe in You can be heavenbound. Amen.

Personal Meditation

...You are the Living Water.

Jesus answered her, "If you knew the gift of God and who it is that asks you for a drink, you would have asked him and he would have given you living water."
John 4:10 (NIV)

Today's Truth:
Jesus is the source of life
for my body and soul.

Living:
ongoing
vital
alive

Prayer of Praise

What You have to offer each of us in this world is an amazing thing—a water that can quench our thirst forever. It is You. When I "drink" from You, I am fulfilled, I experience peace, and I will live victoriously. May many today know You as the Living Water and choose to secure their life in You, drinking deeply of all You are. Amen.

Personal Meditation

...You know all about me.

Then the woman left her waterpot beside the well and went back to the village and told everyone, "Come and meet a man who told me everything I ever did! Can this be the Messiah?" So the people came streaming from the village to see him.
John 4:28-30 (LB)

Many from the Samaritan village believed he was the Messiah because of the woman's report: "He told me everything I ever did!"
John 4:39 (LB)

Today's Truth:
Christ knows us inside out.

Everything:
all aspects
the entirety

Prayer of Praise

How awesome, Lord, that when no one else seems to "get" what I'm feeling or saying, I can know that You understand me totally. Just as people streamed from this woman's village, may people in this world today again stream to You as they discover that You created them, know them, and love them so deeply. Amen.

Personal Meditation

...You are the Bread of Life.

Yes, I am the Bread of Life! When your fathers in the wilderness ate bread from the skies, they all died. But the Bread from heaven gives eternal life to everyone who eats it. I am the Living Bread that came down out of heaven. Anyone eating this Bread shall live forever; this Bread is my flesh given to redeem humanity.
John 6:48-51 (LB)

Today's Truth:
Christ, the Bread of Life,
sustains us through eternity.

Bread:
nourishment
sustenance

Prayer of Praise

I praise You, Father, for as I have partaken of You, my Living Bread...
    I will live eternally.
    I am a member of the body of Christ.
    I am equipped with everything I need in life.
In every land, bread is a staple. So are You, Lord, Jesus! Amen.

...I am one of your sheep.

*"The man who enters by the gate is the shepherd of his sheep.
The watchman opens the gate for him, and the sheep listen to his voice.
He calls his own sheep by name and leads them out."*
John 10:2-4 (NIV)

*Therefore Jesus said again, "I tell you the truth,
I am the gate for the sheep."*
John 10:7 (NIV)

Today's Truth:
God desires us to be easily
led by His voice alone.

Sheep:
regarded as submissive
easily swayed or led

Prayer of Praise

How often I have experienced You, my Shepherd, caring for me as one
of Your sheep, tenderly drawing me to Yourself. You close the "gate" to
sin and relationships that would draw me away from You. I know I can
hear You speaking to me as I read the Bible. Please continue to help me
tune out all other distracting voices and noise and listen only to Your
voice. Amen.

Personal Meditation

...You design life to be lived to the fullest.

"The thief's purpose is to steal, kill and destroy.
My purpose is to give life in all its fullness."
John 10:10 (LB)

Today's Truth:
Though this world can be an ugly place,
with Christ we can experience
a wonderfully satisfying life.

Fullness:
breadth
wholeness
abundance

Prayer of Praise

That verse is so true about You, Jesus. You have given my life so much purpose. The plan You have for me is specially designed for who You've created me to be. You tailor-make the path for each of our lives as we trust in You. I praise You for the fullness my life has because of You. Amen.

Personal Meditation

Day 301

...You gave Your life for me.

"I am the Good Shepherd and know my own sheep, and they know me, just as my Father knows me and I know the Father; and I lay down my life for the sheep."
John 10:14-15 (LB)

"The Father loves me because I lay down my life that I may have it back again."
John 10:17 (LB)

Today's Truth:
Christ knew that laying down His life was necessary, but that He would not be defeated. He would take it up again.

Lay down:
give up
offer

Prayer of Praise

Good Shepherd, You made a way for me to be with You forever. In laying down Your life for me, You offered me everlasting life. What a miracle was performed when You rose up from that grave, taking back Your life again. You are alive today! I praise You that I am able to have fellowship with You this moment and forevermore. Amen.

Personal Meditation

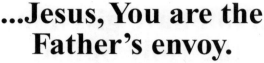

...Jesus, You are the Father's envoy.

The next day, the news that Jesus was on the way to Jerusalem swept through the city, and a huge crowd of Passover visitors took palm branches and went down the road to meet him, shouting, "The Savior! God bless the King of Israel! Hail to God's Ambassador!"
John 12:12-13 (LB)

Today's Truth:

Christ was appointed by God to come to earth to do the work He did. And He did it!

Envoy:
delegate
messenger
representative

Prayer of Praise

Jesus, the Father sent me You—His very best! You are the envoy from God, of the highest rank. There is none greater. You are, as they said, the Savior, the King of Israel, and yes, You alone are God's Ambassador! You have brought to me the good news of Your kingdom, so I, too may be a resident and representative! Amen.

Personal Meditation

...You have given me the Holy Spirit.

If you love me, you will obey what I command.
And I will ask the Father, and he will give you another
Counselor to be with you forever—the Spirit of truth...
John 14:15-17a (NIV)

Today's Truth:

God did not leave His children
empty-handed. He gave us the Holy
Spirit to meet all our needs.

Holy Spirit:

Third Person of Trinity
Comforter
Counselor

Prayer of Praise

Holy Spirit, how often I have asked You to teach me, and You have.
How often I have asked You for help, and You have comforted me. You
give me direction and wisdom. You are a precious gift from the Father.
As You indwell me, I ask You to:

> make God's Word clear to me.
> show me areas in my life I need to change.
> reveal God's mysteries to me.

Amen.

Personal Meditation

...People from every tribe and tongue will declare Your authority.

...that at the name of Jesus every knee should bow, in heaven and on earth and under the earth, and every tongue confess that Jesus Christ is Lord, to the glory of God the Father. Philippians 2:10-11 (NIV)

All the nations you have made will come and worship before you, O Lord; they will bring glory to your name. Psalm 86:9 (NIV)

Today's Truth:
On the day He chooses,
all people will yield to God.

Worship:
applaud
wonder at

Prayer of Praise

What will it be like, Father...to hear everyone who ever lived confess You as Lord—those who were Your servants and those who refused to acknowledge You. It will be a marvelous event when all Your children, from every nation, gather around Your throne and in one voice say,
"Holy is the Lord Almighty!
Worthy is the Lamb that was slain!"
Amen.

Personal Meditation

...You made direct access to God possible.

Now we rejoice in our wonderful new relationship with God—all because of what our Lord Jesus Christ has done in dying for our sins—making us friends of God.
Romans 5:11 (LB)

...Christ's righteousness makes men right with God, so that they can live.
Romans 5:18b (LB)

Today's Truth:
Because of Christ, I can commune with the Father.

Relationship:
alliance
likeness
interrelation

Prayer of Praise

My relationship with God the Father has been made possible through Your dying for my sins and through Your righteousness, dear Jesus. You have made me a friend of God, perfectly upright in His eyes. How wonderful to know that I am cherished by You, and that I have direct access to the Father. Whenever I come in prayer, I know I am being heard. Amen.

Personal Meditation

...You have set me free from sin.

*But now that you have been set free from sin and have
become slaves to God, the benefit you reap leads to holiness,
and the result is eternal life.*
Romans 6:22 (NIV)

Today's Truth:
Sin no longer dictates my life;
I am a servant of the Lord.

Set free:
acquit
release
vindicate

Prayer of Praise

What a blessing to be free from the power of sin! You alone, Lord
Jesus, made that possible through Your death, burial, and resurrection!
You delivered me. You keep me. Your life is within me. I have died
with Christ to the power of sin and have a new nature. What a
transformation! Amen.

Personal Meditation

...You are the One
I will bow to one day.

It is written: "As surely as I live," says the Lord, "every knee will bow before me; every tongue will confess to God."
Romans 14:11 (NIV)

Today's Truth:
God wants me, through my lifestyle, to declare to the world each day that He is God.

Confess:
acknowledge
affirm
declare

Prayer of Praise

You have provided so well for me, Jesus. You are always my Lord... today, tomorrow, forever. I realize that You are Lord for all who know You as their Savior. One day, all people will bow before You and acknowledge You for Who You are and have always been. Amen.

Personal Meditation

...You help me to live peaceably with others.

May God who gives patience, steadiness, and encouragement help you to live in complete harmony with each other—each with the attitude of Christ toward the other.
Romans 15:5 (LB)

Today's Truth:
God wants me to pursue unity and peace.

Harmony:
kinship
cooperation

Prayer of Praise

It is only through Your Holy Spirit, Father, that I am empowered with fruits such as love, peace and patience. When I have relational conflicts, You, Lord, help me to confront and process them in the spirit of Christ's love. Left to myself, I defile You entirely. But You give me spiritual strength and stamina to endure tough times and hard encounters. In moments when I want to fly off the handle or criticize another, You help me refrain and get ahold of a right attitude. You alone, God, consistently help me to be a cheerleader and encourager in others' lives. Amen.

Personal Meditation

...In You, I can have a steady walk.

I commit you to God, who is able to make you strong and steady in the Lord, just as the Gospel says, and just as I have told you.
Romans 16:25 (LB)

Today's Truth:

When I abide in the Lord, I receive power to be stable.

Steady:
regular
continuous

Prayer of Praise

In this world that seems ready to blow apart, You remain unfaltering. In the middle of the uncertainties in my world, I praise You for making me resolute and able. Through You, I can exert influence and make a kingdom difference. I want to cling to You, Lord, and not waver in my commitment to You. Amen.

Personal Meditation

...Your Spirit enlightens me.

We have not received the spirit of the world but the Spirit
who is from God, that we may understand what God has freely given us.
I Corinthians 2:12 (NIV)

Today's Truth:
Through the Spirit at work in my life,
I am informed of the things of God
and edified and uplifted by His Truth.

Enlighten:
advise
give faith

Prayer of Praise

I am so grateful, dear Father, that You have given Your Holy Spirit to make me aware of more of the all of who You are. I can't even imagine how much of You I don't know or understand! But I do understand that You love me and want me to love You back. You ask for obedience, but still You are full of grace. I praise You for giving steady joy to my soul through Your Spirit, my personal Trainer and Sponsor! Amen.

Personal Meditation

...You allow Yourself to be known.

The spiritual man makes judgments about all things, but he himself is not subject to any man's judgment: "For who has known the mind of the Lord that he may instruct him?" But we have the mind of Christ.
I Corinthians 2:15-16 (NIV)

Today's Truth:
Christ makes known to me that which is honoring and pleasing to Him.

Subject:
controlled
bound by

Prayer of Praise

Jesus, to have a share in the very mind of Christ through Your Word and Your Spirit is a most incredible gift. I am so glad that You, Who are governed by no one, choose to share Your heart with Your people, that we may have the same heart. I invite You to examine me and show me how to more consistently bring glory to You. I desire the very mind of Christ to consume me this day. Thank you for that great and precious privilege. Amen.

Personal Meditation

...You allow Your children to find wholeness in You, whether they are single or married.

God gives some the gift of a husband or wife, and others
he gives the gift of being able to stay happily unmarried.
I Corinthians 7:7b (LB)

Today's Truth:

God gives me the capacity to live out His plan
within my own unique situation.

Gift:

blessing
ability
power

Prayer of Praise

I praise You, Father, for Your blessing upon both marriage and singleness. I see couples who make such wonderful teams that it is obvious You designed them to live that way. And I see singles who have beautiful hearts for You and unique opportunities and abilities to do Kingdom work. Whatever the situation, You equip each of us to have an active role and responsibility in Your special plan. Amen.

Personal Meditation

Day 313

...I will one day live beyond my present limitations.

Just as each of us now has a body like Adam's,
so we shall some day have a body like Christ's.
I Corinthians 15:49 (LB)

Today's Truth:
In heaven, I will have a celestial body.
No more aches and pains.

Celestial:
heavenly
spiritual
immortal

Prayer of Praise

What a wonder! How amazing! No more wrinkles... no more
cellulite... no space limitations... a body like Yours, Jesus! Sin will not
be present, so there will be nothing getting in my way. The enjoyment
of the fullness of Christ in a supernatural world will be given to every
believer. I will be entirely free and will experience new phenomena
and levels of communion as I am in the home of the Divine. Amen.

Personal Meditation

...You, Jesus, defeated death!

The sting of death is sin, and the power of sin is the law. But thanks be to God! He gives us the victory through our Lord Jesus Christ.
I Corinthians 15:56-57 (NIV)

Today's Truth:
I can accomplish anything for Christ—through Christ.

Victory:
triumph
ascendancy

Prayer of Praise

How worthy of all praise and adoration You are! You always keep Your Word. You do exactly as You say. You give me victory in Christ. Death is no longer the victor over us. You took away the sting of death, and the law is not my judge! Amen.

Personal Meditation

...My life has meaning.

Such confidence as this is ours through Christ before God.
Not that we are competent in ourselves to claim anything
for ourselves, but our competence comes from God.
2 Corinthians 3:4-5 (NIV)

Today's Truth:
I have great potential
and purpose because of Christ.

Competence:
adequacy
capability
qualification

Prayer of Praise

All that I now am and ever hope to be, dear Jesus, is because of
You. You give me the ability to act and prosper. You alone give me
everlasting life. Through You I can bring glory to God. I praise You for
these special talents and spiritual gifts. Help me to do everything I do
as unto You. Amen.

Personal Meditation

...You shine Your light through me.

But this precious treasure—this light and power that now shine within us—is held in a perishable container, that is, in our weak bodies. Everyone can see the glorious power within must be from God and is not our own.
2 Corinthians 4:7 (LB)

Today's Truth:
God shares His power, beauty
and light with me.

Treasure:
prize
valuable

Prayer of Praise

Father, You are the Light in my soul! You light up my life, illuminating the dark side and bringing me wholeness and forgiveness. You shine through my imperfection and allow others to see Your light in spite of who I am. Thank You for loving and empowering me. I want to be a help to others, not a hindrance. I want to demonstrate in my life each day who You are. Amen.

Personal Meditation

...When I come to You with my sorrow and suffering, You teach me and You touch my heart.

Godly sorrow brings repentance that leads to salvation and leaves no regret, but worldly sorrow brings death.
2 Corinthians 7:10 (NIV)

Today's Truth:
Mourning over my disobedience and defilement of God humbles me and causes me to repent.

Sorrow:
grieving
remorse

Prayer of Praise

During the times when I am in distress over the ways I let You down, You turn my chin up to look into Your face and hear You speak. You tell me that I have sinned and I have let You down, but You never leave me in this place. You also remind me that I can grow through my experiences. But more than anything, You assure me of Your love for me. Thank You for purifying times of godly sorrow. Amen.

Personal Meditation

...Father, You gave me the indescribable gift of Your Son.

Thank God for his Son—his Gift too wonderful for words.
2 Corinthians 9:15 (LB)

Today's Truth:
Jesus is God's gift to me—my personal
Savior and Advocate sent from the Father.

Indescribable:
amazing
unexplainable

Prayer of Praise

Dear Father, what an unspeakably precious Gift You gave... Your only Son. It is true; it is too wonderful for words. My words of worship, wonder, and praise do not begin to speak my heart. You gave Your only Son to provide a way to heaven—and to You. In Christ, Your Son—sin, death, hell, and Satan were all defeated. Amen.

Personal Meditation

...You live in me.

*I have been crucified with Christ: and I myself no longer live,
but Christ lives in me. And the real life I now have within this
body is a result of my trusting in the Son of God,
who loved me and gave himself for me.*
Galatians 2:20 (LB)

Today's Truth:
Because of Christ, I don't have to
obey my sinful nature.

Trust:
reliance
faith
confidence

Prayer of Praise

You gave Yourself for me, Jesus, without anything in exchange—no
price to pay on my part. You did it all. I asked, and You came into my
life. It is all about You, Jesus. Your very life is my life! You live in me
by Your Holy Spirit. It is not the "old" me that now lives, but it is the
"new" me. I am Your child. Amen.

Personal Meditation

...Through Christ I am an heir to all that God has promised His people.

And now that we are Christ's we are true descendants of Abraham, and all of God's promises to him belong to us.
Galatians 3:29 (LB)

Today's Truth:
God is my hope. I stand on His promises.

Expectation:
anticipation
trust

Prayer of Praise

Your Word is rich with personal promises for me! Promises:
    to never leave me
    of heaven
    of Your coming
    of Your faithful, every-moment love
I praise You for being the Author and Keeper of these precious promises. Amen.

Personal Meditation

...You are my Father Who bestows favor and blessing.

How we praise God, the Father of our Lord Jesus Christ, who has blessed us with every blessing in heaven because we belong to Christ.
Ephesians 1:3 (LB)

Today's Truth:
God enriches my life with every blessing—
the greatest of which is Christ.

Favor:
blessing
grace
kindness

Prayer of Praise

How do I begin the list of all my blessings?!
Blessings of...
      nature
      family
      health
I praise You for being the God who blesses so abundantly and freely.
Amen.

Personal Meditation

...I am Your artwork!

For we are God's workmanship, created in Christ Jesus to do good works,
which God prepared in advance for us to do.
Ephesians 2:10 (NIV)

Today's Truth:
God created me to do good works
and to advance His Kingdom.

Workmanship:
handiwork
expertise

Prayer of Praise

Father, I am not sure where the saying comes from, but I know it is
true: GOD DOES NOT MAKE JUNK! To ponder the thought that I
am created in Your image is so amazing. It is humbling to consider that
I have been directed by God Himself to do good works—to bring glory
to Your name and to live my life in a Christ-like manner. Oh, may I
freely tell others so they too may worship and praise You, and one day
be like You. Amen.

Personal Meditation

...You provide for and work within me far beyond my highest hope.

*Now glory be to God who by his mighty power at work within us
is able to do far more than we would dare to ask or even dream
of—infinitely beyond our highest prayers, desires, thoughts, or hopes.*
Ephesians 3:20 (LB)

Today's Truth:

By God's mighty power in me, He is able
to accomplish His purpose for my life in
ways I can't even imagine.

Sufficient:
plentiful
acceptable

Prayer of Praise

Your work within me truly is beyond:
>   my greatest prayer.
>   any desires I have.
>   my thoughts of a mighty God.
>   my hope of what is yet to be mine

There is no need that I will have today that You are not able to meet.
Amen.

Personal Meditation

...You indwell and live through me.

For us there is only one Lord, one faith, one baptism,
and we all have the same God and Father who is over us all and in us all,
and living through every part of us.
Ephesians 4:5-6 (LB)

Today's Truth:
I am justified in placing my faith in one
God—the Father living in me.

Faith:
belief
conviction
confidence

Prayer of Praise

Lord Jesus, may I "wear" You as the finest fragrance—that others will become a "sweet aroma" to You when they accept You as their Savior. Because You provided a way to heaven, Jesus, by dying on the cross for my sins, we share the same Father! I am adopted, through salvation, into Your family. You have made me a "joint-heir" with YOU. You, Jesus, live through every part of me today. Amen.

Personal Meditation

...Jesus, You are the precise representation of the Father to me.

Christ is the exact likeness of the unseen God.
He existed before God made anything at all...
Colossians 1:15 (LB)

Today's Truth:
If I know Christ, I know the Father.

Likeness:
depiction
resemblance

Prayer of Praise

Before the world was made, Christ existed. You are a God who never tires, never grows old, never needs an operation, has perfect vision and for Whom arthritis will never be a problem. You will always remain pure. Amen.

Personal Meditation

...You give meaning to all of Your creation.

For by him all things were created: things in heaven and on earth, visible and invisible, whether thrones or powers or rulers or authorities; all things were created by him and for him. He is before all things, and in him all things hold together.
Colossians 1:16-17 (NIV)

Today's Truth:
All creation finds its purpose and unity in God, the Creator of the universe.

Hold:
keep
bind

Prayer of Praise

Absolutely everything—
    on the earth
    under the earth
    in the heavens
Everything exists for Your use and for Your glory. BE GLORIFIED, LORD JESUS CHRIST! Wholly and entirely, You give meaning and cohesiveness to all You have created. Amen.

Personal Meditation

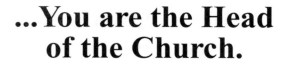

...You are the Head of the Church.

And he is the head of the body, the church; he is the beginning and the firstborn
from among the dead, so that in everything he might have the supremacy.
For God was pleased to have all his fullness dwell in him.
Colossians 1:18-19 (NIV)

Today's Truth:
Christ is Lord of all.

Supremacy:
absolute rule
dominion
lordship

Prayer of Praise

What a perfect Leader! You are:
- holy
- blameless
- faithful
- powerful
- wise
- dependable
- loving

I willingly follow You, my Lord. In You alone I can realize fullness–
enduring completeness–in my life! Amen.

Personal Meditation

Day 330

...You gave Your Son Jesus Christ to bring peace and joy to our troubled world.

It was through what his Son did that God cleared a path for everything to come to him—all things in heaven and on earth—for Christ's death on the cross has made peace with God for all by his blood.
Colossians 1:20a (LB)

Today's Truth:
Christ is my Way-Maker, making peace and direct communion with God possible.

Foremost:
chief
preeminent
supreme

Prayer of Praise

Jesus, You are the first in everything! No one has wisdom like You. No one sees all things clearly as You do. No one loves perfectly as You do. And through You, the Father has reconciled and invited all to come to Him and receive everlasting peace. Amen.

Personal Meditation

...You reached out to me.

Once you were alienated from God and were enemies in your minds because of your evil behavior. But now he has reconciled you by Christ's physical body through death to present you holy in his sight, without blemish and free from accusation...
Colossians 1:21-22 (NIV)

Today's Truth:
God gladly picks me up and out of my selfish mire and washes me white as snow.

Reconcile:
bring together
reunite
mediate

Prayer of Praise

Jesus, You left no one out! You made a way to heaven for all people, no matter where they live, no matter their skin color, no matter their language! The price You paid to make this possible, I know I will never fully comprehend. But I do know that only You, Jesus, could be a sufficient sacrifice for my sin. Amen.

Personal Meditation

...In You I find all the understanding I'll ever need.

*In him lie hidden all the mighty, untapped treasures
of wisdom and knowledge.*
Colossians 2:3 (LB)

Today's Truth:
God shares with me
things unknown to this world.

Hidden:
concealed
unseen
veiled

Prayer of Praise

I give You all my praise for revealing the secret of salvation. As I grow in You, I give you my praise for revealing more and more of Your wisdom and knowledge to me. I know that in You are unlimited resources I can tap into as I strive to walk closely with You. For today, be all my Wisdom. For today, give me the understanding I will need to make manifest your vast goodness in my needy world. Amen.

Personal Meditation

...You have all authority and power.

For in Christ there is all of God in a human body; so you have everything when you have Christ, and you are filled with God through your union with Christ. He is the highest Ruler, with authority over every other power.
Colossians 2:9-10 (LB)

Today's Truth:
As I stand united with Christ, I stand in the fullness of God's power.

Union:
incorporation
conciliation

Prayer of Praise

Through You, Jesus, I have direct access to God the Father. It is a perfect union—You've provided all I will ever need. As I look at my world today, there are leaders who believe they have great power and authority, but none has more than (or are in any way equal to) You, Jesus! Amen.

Personal Meditation

...Having You, Jesus, is all that matters.

In this new life one's nationality or race or education or social position is unimportant; such things mean nothing. Whether a person has Christ is what matters, and he is equally available to all.
Colossians 3:11 (LB)

Today's Truth:
Yes, spiritually speaking, it is who you know that counts!

Available:
attainable
useable
open to

Prayer of Praise

Lord Jesus, whatever the time or circumstance, You are always there, waiting for me to come to You. You share in my joys, in my crises, and in my needs. I give You all my praise. I'm so glad that it doesn't matter to You how much money I have or how successful I am! You are there, waiting for me ALL THE TIME! It matters only that I know and walk with You. Amen.

Personal Meditation

...I am beloved by You.

We know that God has chosen you, dear brothers,
much beloved of God.
1 Thessalonians 1:4 (LB)

Today's Truth:
God has chosen to love me.

Chosen:
elected
selected

Prayer of Praise

What joy, Father, to be invited to share Your glory in heaven! What a day that will be when I see You face to face. I will bow down and worship the One who died for me! You knew all about me before I was born, and You scheduled every day of my life before even one came to be (Ps. 139:16). Some of my days I would not choose to live over, but praise You, Jesus, Your hand was always there to guide me. Amen.

Personal Meditation

...Your Word changed my life.

And we also thank God continually because, when you received
the word of God, which you heard from us, you accepted it not as
the word of men, but as it actually is, the word of God,
which is at work in you who believe.
1 Thessalonians 2:13 (NIV)

Today's Truth:
God's Word is life-changing for those
who are seeking to grow.

Accept:
receive
believe
trust

Prayer of Praise

Father, Your Word encourages and strengthens me as I live each day. It
has changed my life in so many ways, such as my:
- behavior
- speech
- thoughts
- friends
- goals
- desires

For these things I give You praise. Amen.

Personal Meditation

...You are coming back to this earth to take Your Church to heaven!

For the Lord himself will come down from heaven... And the believers who are dead will be the first to rise to meet the Lord. Then we who are still alive and remain on the earth will be caught up with them in the clouds to meet the Lord in the air and remain with him forever.
1 Thessalonians 4:16-17 (LB)

Today's Truth

Jesus will one day personally escort us to the home He has been preparing for us, His Bride.

Church:
The Body of Christ
Believers everywhere

Prayer of Praise

You are coming back soon! Yes, You will return in the same way You went to heaven and Your Bride, the Church, will rise to meet You! It is hard to wait. How amazing to realize that whether our bodies are dead or we are alive when You return, we will all come up to meet You and then forever be with You! Come soon, Lord Jesus! Amen.

Personal Meditation

Day 338

...You help me understand how to know You.

Oh, how kind our Lord was, for he showed me how to trust him and become full of the love of Christ Jesus.
1 Timothy 1:14 (LB)

Today's Truth:

We are not capable of knowing/ understanding God on our own. He is the light by which we see the Light.

Full:
abounding in
complete

Prayer of Praise

You do not just give me Your grace and love, but You POUR it out! It is an endless stream and an endless flow. When I did not deserve Your love, while I was yet a sinner, You died for me. You, Jesus, even showed me how to trust You. All that I have, and all that I am is because of You. Amen.

Personal Meditation

...You abundantly supply so many things for my pleasure.

Command those who are rich in this present world not to be arrogant nor to put their hope in wealth, which is so uncertain, but to put their hope in God, who richly provides us with everything for our enjoyment.
I Timothy 6:17 (NIV)

Today's Truth:

God knows what pursuits are truly enjoyable and loves to give us these things as we hope in Him.

Richly:
suitably
generously

Prayer of Praise

Father, how I praise You for Your plan, that even though you created us to live only a few short years on this earth, You wanted it to be a lifetime of knowing You and experiencing Your blessings. You give to Your children in such abundance, going beyond our daily needs and offering us so many pleasurable things and experiences as well. Amen.

Personal Meditation

...You come through for me.

If we are faithless, he will remain faithful,
for he cannot disown himself.
2 Timothy 2:13 (NIV)

Today's Truth
Even when we are struggling to believe, God gives us the strength to hold onto our faith in Him.

Disown:
refuse to acknowledge ownership
abandon

Prayer of Praise

There may be circumstances or situations that arise today, Jesus, that I will have little or no faith to walk as I should. It is wonderful to know that it won't be left solely up to me or my abilities. You will work through me and only require that I trust in You. Thank you for being faithful to me all the time! Amen.

Personal Meditation

Day 341

...You promise Your servants and equip them with faith and knowledge.

Paul, a servant of God and an apostle of Jesus Christ for the faith of God's elect and the knowledge of the truth that leads to godliness— a faith and knowledge resting on the hope of eternal life, which God, who does not lie, promised before the beginning of time.
Titus 1:1-2 (NIV)

Godliness:
righteousness
holiness

Today's Truth:
God cannot lie.

Prayer of Praise

When I come to You in prayer and when I read Your Word, there is never an untrue statement or false impression. You faithfully lead Your children to Truth. It's not hard to understand how I can trust You, Lord, for from You can only come that which is absolutely true. Continue to deepen my faith and increase my knowledge of You. Amen.

Personal Meditation

...You, Jesus, rescued me from my sinful nature.

He died under God's judgment against our sins, so that he could rescue us from constant falling into sin and make us his very own people, with cleansed hearts and real enthusiasm for doing kind things for others.
Titus 2:14 (LB)

Today's Truth:
Christ was obedient to death
on the cross for us.

Cleansed:
free from moral guilt
free from blemish
purify

Prayer of Praise

Lord, I am Your very own! You were willing to come under Your Father's judgment against sin to become sin for me. You have put it into my heart to do kindnesses to others. Today, Jesus, strengthen and motivate me, by the power of Your Spirit, to express Your love more unconditionally to those about me. Use me today to share You freely—I want my actions to demonstrate that You are on the throne of my heart. Amen.

Personal Meditation

...You are in command of everything.

For though you made him lower than the angels for a little while, now you have crowned him with glory and honor. And you have put him in complete charge of everything there is. Nothing is left out.
Hebrews 2:7-8 (LB)

Today's Truth:
There is no person, country, threat, situation, or event that is "above" God. He is over all.

Charge:
authority
duty

Prayer of Praise

You are in charge of everything—
    the birds when it is time to fly south.
    the continual beating of my heart.
    the squirrels as they store acorns for winter.
    the growth of a baby into a child.
    the direction of the wind.
    Nothing is left out. Amen.

Personal Meditation

...You are a perfect Leader.

And it was right and proper that God, who made everything for his own glory, should allow Jesus to suffer, for in doing this he was bringing vast multitudes of God's people to heaven; for his suffering made Jesus a perfect Leader, one fit to bring them into their salvation.
Hebrews 2:10 (LB)

Today's Truth:
Jesus' suffering and death gives me Life
today and every day.

Fit:
thoroughly qualified
equipped

Prayer of Praise

In Your suffering You have brought masses of people to salvation. You, Jesus, meet all the requirements to be a great leader. Because You became flesh, You are now my perfect mediator to God the Father. You said to the Father faithfully, "...yet not what I will, but what you will." (Mark 14:36b) When suffering comes to me, may I also be able to say, "Not my will, but Yours be done." Amen.

Personal Meditation

...You understand the temptations I face.

For since he himself has now been through suffering and temptation, he knows what it is like when we suffer and are tempted, and he is wonderfully able to help us.
Hebrews 2:18 (LB)

Today's Truth:
God will never fail to give us the strength to overcome both small and large temptations if we seek Him for help.

Temptation:
persuasion for me to do wrong
enticement

Prayer of Praise

You are so able to help me when I am tempted and suffer, because You also have been through temptation and suffering and know exactly what I am going through. You are not only able to help me when I suffer or when I am tempted, but You are able to deliver me from it. So I will confidently ask for help in my time of temptation. Amen.

Personal Meditation

...You instruct me as to how to live.

Keep your eyes on Jesus, our leader and instructor. He was willing to die a shameful death on the cross because of the joy he knew would be his afterwards; and now he sits in the place of honor by the throne of God.
Hebrews 12:2 (LB)

Today's Truth:
As I fix my eyes on Christ, He shows me the path He wants me to take.

Instructor:
one who imparts knowledge
demonstrator

Prayer of Praise

As my Guide, You give me specific instructions on how to live my life. I will keep looking to You, Jesus, as I patiently run the race You have for me. What a day that will be, Jesus, as I stand with all Your children around the throne of God... singing praises to You, Who faithfully led and guided us throughout each of our lives. Amen.

Personal Meditation

...Your correction is perfect.

*Our earthly fathers trained us for a few brief years,
doing the best for us that they knew how, but God's
correction is always right and for our best good, that we
may share his holiness.*
Hebrews 12:10 (LB)

Today's Truth:
God takes great care in the upbringing
of His children.

Correction:
discipline
reproof

Prayer of Praise

You desire that I share Your holiness, so You:
    chasten me when I need it,
    free me from my mistakes,
    make right my errors.
As my Father, I praise You for correcting me in just the right ways.
You know…
    when I need mercy,
    when I need to feel Your presence,
    when I need to be admonished.
You parent me perfectly! Amen.

Personal Meditation

...You remain the same.

Jesus Christ is the same yesterday
and today and forever.
Hebrews 13:8 (NIV)

Today's Truth:
God has never wavered in character
throughout all of history and never will.

Same:
unchanged

Prayer of Praise

How many times have I heard people say that change is good...get
used to change... what was today will not be tomorrow. But I rest in
the console of You, Father, the UNchangeable One!! You are a comfort
to me in an always-changing world. Thank You for staying exactly the
same. Amen.

Personal Meditation

...You give us spiritual leaders to watch and guide our steps.

Obey your spiritual leaders and be willing to do what they say. For their work is to watch over your souls, and God will judge them on how well they do this. Give them reason to report joyfully about you to the Lord and not with sorrow, for then you will suffer for it too."
Hebrews 13:17 (LB)

Today's Truth:
I am accountable to God
and His overseers.

Leader:
head
shepherd
counselor

Prayer of Praise

I praise You for providing me with wisdom and knowledge to lead others. I want to lay the gift of leadership at Your feet, Jesus, and ask You to help me obey You wherever You lead me. There are times when both leading and following are difficult and even lonely. Please put in our hearts the passion to love You deeply enough to obey fully. Amen.

Personal Meditation

...You give wisdom generously to those who seek it.

If you want to know what God wants you to do, ask him, and he will gladly tell you, for he is always ready to give a bountiful supply of wisdom to all who ask him; he will not resent it.
James 1:5 (LB)

Today's Truth:
God is eager to provide for His children the character-gifts that are truly helpful.

Bountiful:
plentiful
generous

Prayer of Praise

I have experienced such joy, Father, as I have been equipped by You for what You have called me to do. I remember saying to You, "Who me, Lord?!" You answered right back, "I will equip you with all you need to do My will." And so You have! Amen.

Personal Meditation

...You are the Source of the wonderful things that come to me.

Every good and perfect gift is from above, coming down from the Father of the heavenly lights, who does not change like shifting shadows.
James 1:17 (NIV)

Today's Truth:

God is good all the time and loves to bless His children.

Source:

giver
author
cause

Prayer of Praise

Because Your Son, who is my Light, shines and lives within me, so much good has come to me. I love that You always have my best interests in mind and are, because of Your character, a good God, in Whom there is no variation or shifting shadow. Amen.

Personal Meditation

...You have given me Your very own Spirit that teaches me how to live in You!

But you have received the Holy Spirit and he lives within you, in your hearts, so that you don't need anyone to teach you what is right. For he teaches you all things, and he is the Truth, and no liar; and so, just as he has said, you must live in Christ, never to depart from him. 1 John 2:27 (LB)

Today's Truth:

Because Christ lives in me, I can know right from wrong.

Teach:
impart knowledge
give instruction
nurture

Prayer of Praise

Oh Holy Spirit, how I praise You for leading me only into what is true. Like Jesus, You also are Truth. Keep teaching me Your Truth so I can easily detect what is false. My world tries to persuade me of so many wrong, twisted things. I want to know what is true and right. Amen.

Personal Meditation

Day 361

...life in You continues forever.

And this is the testimony: God has given us eternal life,
and this life is in his Son.
1 John 5:11 (NIV)

Today's Truth:
In Christ there is Life...Life eternal

Testimony:
proclamation
affirmation
proof

Prayer of Praise

It is true, I know it is true! Jesus, You are God's beloved Son! In You I
have all I need for life. In You is joy unspeakable. In You is peace in the
middle of chaos. You are my life, my joy, my peace. Amen.

Personal Meditation

...You protect me from Satan.

We know that anyone born of God does not continue to sin;
the one who was born of God keeps him safe,
and the evil one cannot harm him.
1 John 5:18 (NIV)

Today's Truth:
God fights for us and gives us tools to
fight our adversary, Satan.

Safe:
secure
shielded

Prayer of Praise

Satan will never have victory over me if I cling to You, Jesus. I know
that You gladly guard and strengthen all those who seek You. Because
of You in me, Satan will not prevail in my life. Amen.

Personal Meditation

...You discipline me in love.

Those whom I love I rebuke and discipline. So be earnest, and repent.
Revelation 3:19 (NIV)

Today's Truth:
When the Lord admonishes me,
it is for my good.

Rebuke:
reprimand
correct

Prayer of Praise

Sometimes the experiences of life that are most difficult have drawn
me the closest to You, Jesus. As You discipline me, Father, may I come
forth looking more and more like Your precious Son, my Savior—the
Lord Jesus Christ. Amen.

Personal Meditation

...You never stop seeking the lost.

*Look! I have been standing at the door and I am
constantly knocking. If anyone hears me calling
him and opens the door, I will come in and
fellowship with him and he with me.*
Revelation 3:20 (LB)

Today's Truth:
God desires me to have a close,
continuing love-relationship with Him.

Constantly:
faithfully
continually

Prayer of Praise

To think, Heavenly Father, that the Creator of all wants my fellowship.
I humbly bow in worship, grateful that You never stopped knocking at
the door of my heart...You are indeed my Savior! You are resolute in
wanting the lost to be Your children. Use me to help those who don't
know You as Savior to find You and receive Your love. Amen.

Personal Meditation

...You are the free Gift of Life itself.

The Spirit and the bride say, "Come!" And let him who hears say, "Come!" Whoever is thirsty, let him come; and whoever wishes, let him take the free gift of the water of life.
Revelation 22:17 (NIV)

Today's Truth:

With open arms, God invites each of us to come and experience Him.

Come:
draw near
enter
attain

Prayer of Praise

Sweet Jesus, You are Lord and King. You are the Beginning and the End. You are the Creator and Sustainer. You are Almighty and Powerful...yet, You live within my heart; I am Your child. I humble myself before You and invite You to show me more of Who You are and how I can be like You. It is with great joy and thanksgiving that I come to You, the bright Morning Star (Revelation 22:16b).

Personal Meditation